"When Joy Jones speaks, the audience listens—and learns. Jones brings her skill and know-how as public speaker, performer, and slam-poetry coach to this lively, informative guide. Tips and playful exercises guide nervous teens to greater confidence, whether speaking in a classroom, off the cuff, or in competition. I wish I had this when I was a teen!"

—MARY QUATTLEBAUM,
children's author and creative writing professor

"I am a visual artist and art educator and often lead talented teens in designing and executing creative products and commissions. These teens often have to present their design concepts in front of clients. The fear is real. This comprehensive and rich book is written in a style that teens can relate to and gives them the tools they need to be successful. I can't wait to recommend this book to my teens."

—ADJOA BURROWES,
author and illustrator

"Joy Jones' advice to young speech makers in *Fearless Public Speaking: A Teen's Guide to Public Speaking* combines hilarious double-takes along with solid examples of how to avoid being boring, ways of using nervousness as an inspiration, and, thankfully, dynamic and stimulating ways to use props and other audiovisuals aids. Each of her chapters—from 'Public Speaking's Greatest Hits' to 'When You Are Not the Speaker: Listening'—-gives concrete exercises for young people to captivate their audiences with their words. My favorite is Joy's exercise for creating new similes and teasing out metaphors to enhance speeches. Joy Jones' *Fearless Public Speaking* is perceptive about young people. I can almost hear their youthful laughter as they read this encouraging text. While they are smiling over Joy's witty statements, they are learning how to make good speeches.

—CAROLIVIA HERRON,
author and professor

FEARLESS PUBLIC SPEAKING

A Guide for Beginners

BY JOY JONES

*sparknotes

ISBN 978-1-4549-3181-2

Distributed in Canada by Sterling Publishing Co., Inc.
c/o Canadian Manda Group, 664 Annette Street
Toronto, Ontario M6S 2C8, Canada
Distributed in the United Kingdom by GMC Distribution Services
Castle Place, 166 High Street, Lewes, East Sussex BN7 1XU, England
Distributed in Australia by NewSouth Books
University of New South Wales, Sydney, NSW 2052, Australia

For information about custom editions, special sales, and premium and corporate purchases, please contact Sterling Special Sales at 800-805-5489 or specialsales@sterlingpublishing.com.

Manufactured in Canada

Lot #:
2 4 6 8 10 9 7 5 3 1
04/19

sterlingpublishing.com
sparknotes.com

Contents

ACKNOWLEDGMENTS

I've been inspired, entertained, and mentored by
some fine speakers: Baba-C, Tania Bond, C. R Gibbs,
Linda Hopper, Lamar McClain, Betty McCloud,
Mary Thomas Newsom, and Addison Switzer.
Thanks to the Millay Colony for the Arts and the
Mid-Atlantic Arts Foundation, where this book got its start.

INTRODUCTION:
Speaking in Public—Why Do It?

That which we are capable of feeling, we are capable of saying.
—*Cervantes*

Suppose you were a teacher and you had to present a geography lesson to your class—but you had to teach it one student at a time. You'd have to repeat that same lesson 20 or 30 times. Suppose the president wanted to tell each citizen about a new tax law—if done one-on-one, that explanation would be given 6.1 million times to the residents in the Washington, D.C., metropolitan area alone.

Now you know why public speaking was invented.

Public speaking is useful and necessary, and better than that, it's fun. Yes, I said fun! I know a lot of you would rather eat fried rat, sleep with snakes, or attend school twelve months a year than appear before an audience. Polls have shown that public speaking is the number one fear of many people. But if you keep reading, you'll find out that public speaking is nothing to be afraid of. In fact, you can enjoy doing it, and I'm going to show you how. Believe it or not, the so-called fear part of it is part of the fun.

I love it when people overcome their speech fright, and I relish seeing a speaker in action. I used to coach a teen poetry slam team. And they were fearless. When I say fearless, do I mean that they were never nervous? No. But they had something to share, and they were so enthusiastic about sharing it that the part of them that was fearful was eclipsed by the part of them that was having fun.

Have you ever held a full-time job, applied for a credit card, driven a truck, been to college, voted for mayor, gotten married, bought a house, or skipped class? Probably not. But those may be things that you're looking forward to doing. And you'll probably do them well. Add giving a speech to that list (but delete skipping class!).

Do you know how to tie your shoelaces, walk to the store alone, send an e-mail, download music, do fractions, and skip class? These are all things that at one time you had never tried before, but now you can do them easily without thinking about them (but hopefully not skipping class. Do not ever think about doing that!). That's the way you'll soon feel about giving a speech.

Speech *Giving?*

What exactly are you *giving* when you *give* a speech? How would you like having the power to influence someone's behavior, make them roar with laughter, or come to a new and better understanding of something? What could be more marvelous than to be the spark that makes that imaginary lightbulb turn on over a person's brain? Often, that's precisely what happens when you speak. When you give a speech you give others a chance to learn, to be entertained, and to see another view. That's the gift you give when you give a speech.

You're also giving *you*—a part of yourself. When you speak you share your thoughts. Others get to witness the distinct way you put ideas together, how your mind works, and what you consider important. Wouldn't it be great to be able to receive a gift that is intriguing, unique, and remarkable? Well, you are intriguing, you are unique, and you are remarkable. When you stand before an audience to speak they get to discover this, too. Even if you didn't know that before I told you so, you'll start to feel that way once you deliver your speech. That's the gift *you* receive when you give a speech.

Presents, Presents, Presents

Ordinary people (that is, those people who aren't lucky enough to be public speakers) only get presents a few times a year. On their birthdays, maybe on a holiday, and perhaps when their grandparents go out of town and bring them back a T-shirt that shrinks the first time they wash it.

But a speaker gets so many good things from speaking. If you can learn to like public speaking, you will eliminate a lot of stress and fear from your life. You won't have to run and hide when the teacher is looking for volunteers to lead the assembly program. You won't have to hunch down behind Billy Martinez when the teacher is scanning the room looking for someone to call on. You won't have to miss out on the enjoyment of speaking.

My slam poets could make the adults in the audience go *"Aww"* when they said something cute or wise. And the kids in the audience would go "Wow!" when they rapped something deep or clever. That's a lot of feel-good! I, too, adore stepping out in front of a group. The larger, the better. I can actually feel waves of energy washing over me as I face the audience. That energy is love. Nearly every occasion to speak is an opportunity to be in love.

Stop shaking your head at what sounds like hype. You, too, can receive the gift of love, public-speaking-style, just as soon as you discover how to relax when you recite. You—yes, you—can definitely proceed from meek to unique when you speak.

Becoming comfortable talking before a group will make you rich and beautiful. Okay, okay, now I'm exaggerating, but there *are* benefits. Speaking boosts self-assurance. When everyone is listening to what you have to say, you just might feel as if you are rich and beautiful. It can lead to better marks on your report card, it will definitely be a beneficial skill when you enter the working world, and lots of people will admire you for it. Those are pretty good reasons for learning how to speak, don't you think?

I hope I've convinced you that learning how to be a better public speaker is worthwhile. Even if I haven't—keep reading! This book is here to show you that it's not as scary as it may seem. And I'm here with you on that enjoyable journey to find your voice.

"Enthusiasm moves the world."
—*Arthur Balfour*

CHAPTER 1
Public Speaking's Greatest Hits

L et's see . . . what's my favorite form of public speaking? That would be hard to say. Currently, I am a performance poet with a group called The Spoken Word. We do poetry, percussion, songs, and storytelling. Entertaining people is something I find extremely gratifying. I also conduct training workshops where I teach, usually in workplace settings, on topics such as communications skills, employment skills, and stress management. I like the exchange of ideas in the room and helping people learn practical things that they can put to use immediately. Cultural and historical lectures are among my most enjoyable speaking engagements. I focus on topics and people that most people don't know about. These lectures also allow me to be creative—although still factual— in how I present the information. I've also been an actor and a teacher. The great thing about acting is that you get applause after you've finished your job. It's like getting a good report card every time. The great thing about being a teacher is you're no longer the one getting a report card.

I can't pick one as my favorite, because each one is fun. So let's take a look at several types of public speaking that you might have fun doing, too.

TYPES OF PUBLIC SPEAKING

Class Participation

It's one thing to know the right answer. It's another to say the answer out loud in front of everybody. Being able to confidently speak up will get you more attention (the good kind) from your instructor, and will probably improve your grade. Class participation also helps you to remember what is being taught more easily. If you have thought *and* talked about an idea, those concepts get more firmly imprinted in your mind. School is more appealing when you take an active role in what's going on.

For example, if you are studying the Second Amendment, the right to bear arms, asking a question might influence a classmate's (or teacher's) opinion. Or, as you listen to the answer to your question, you may get a perspective you didn't have previously. In any event, when it's time to take the test, the conversation and reflection you have done in class will have prepared you to do well on the test.

Oral Report

Presenting a report on a book you've read, explaining your work at the blackboard, giving a detailed explanation of an event or lesson—these are all examples of oral reports. The student is giving information that he or she has studied and is demonstrating knowledge of the topic. Oral reports can be informal and impromptu, such as when you're asked to go to the board, or planned and prepared, as in a book review. You've done this type of report before, haven't you? Even the youngest students have given oral reports when they present a favorite toy or introduce the class to their pet at Show and Tell. See, you're more experienced than you thought.

Informational Speech

This type of speech is exactly what it sounds like: one that gives out information. A talk about the different types of cloud formations, how to score a football game, the history of hip hop—all are informational speeches. Most lessons teachers present are basically informational speeches, so you've had a lot of experience being on the receiving end of these sorts of speeches. Delivering an informational speech mostly requires that you be organized and factual. If you've ever provided directions to a lost person, taught your baby brother how to lace his sneakers, explained how to do a lay-up, or told a classmate what it takes to get an A in Mrs. Moy's class, then you've already given an informational speech one-on-one. Doing it in front of a group will be a snap.

Persuasive Speech

"Mom, please let me go to the movies, puh-leeze? Everybody else is going, and it's a really good movie, so you should let me go, too. Okay?" This is an attempt at a persuasive speech— not a very good attempt, but you get the picture! Persuasive speech is a type of speaking you've also tried, one where you try to convince others to change their opinion, behavior, or point of view. When the outcome of a situation is critical, persuasive speaking becomes a pivotal skill to have. If you are a competent speaker there is an excellent chance that you can get people to support your point of view. Good times to use this type of speech might be when there is a move to make school year-round, when the school is trying to change policies on cell phone use, or when you or a classmate is running for office.

When I was in sixth grade, I, among several other students, ran for student council. Our teacher asked each candidate to give a short speech explaining why he or she was the best person for the job. When it was my turn, I simply said, "My classmates know who I am. I don't need to convince anybody." Bad move. I lost. Everyone else made a pitch that showcased their good qualities. I should have taken the opportunity to shine a light on my talents, to be persuasive. The outcome might have been different.

Dramatic Recitation

Dramatic recitation could be anything from reciting a poem by a famous writer, competing in a poetry slam with one of your own rap originals, or reading an excerpt from a play or novel. With a work of this type, you don't just read it aloud, you have to interpret it. The way you say the words has to bring them to life so that the listeners sense the emotions, see the colors, feel the sensations, and fully experience the message of the piece. Dramatic recitation usually requires some acting skill in addition to good platform skills. People who are good at dramatic readings leave their audiences touched—sometimes even transformed.

Debate

Debate is persuasive speaking extreme. Debaters select or are assigned an issue to explain and defend. These issues, often called *arguments*, must be researched, and the facts that support the position must be logically presented. Speakers are usually organized on teams and compete against one another, and there are strict time and format procedures that must be followed when posing or defending an argument. A fierce debate can be as exciting to watch as a hard-fought sports event. These are some current topics on the circuit: Performance-enhancing drugs—should they be allowed in sports? Should visible tattoos be allowed in the workplace? Is human cloning desirable or dangerous? Should employers judge employees by their social media accounts? Single-sex schools—are they a good idea or not?

Master of Ceremonies

The master ceremonies, or MC, is a combination traffic cop and a DJ without any music. He or she introduces each part of a program, makes sure the program keeps flowing, and keeps the audience interested in the proceedings. MCs host a wide range of programs: school assemblies, talent shows, awards presentations, parties, and receptions. Although an MC may read his or her remarks off a script, sometimes the MC will have to ad-lib, or make up comments on the spot, to fill time when the next group or individual on the agenda is delayed or there is some other glitch. An MC needs to be quick-thinking—and a sense of humor doesn't hurt, either.

Extemporaneous and Impromptu Speaking

Sometimes you're asked to speak on the spur of the moment with no or very little time for preparation or notes to guide you. This is extemporaneous or impromptu speaking. Can you come up with something intelligent to say? Of course you can! Everyday situations can become occasions when impromptu speaking is required. Perhaps the speaker you invited to a Spanish club meeting doesn't show. Maybe at Thanksgiving dinner, each family member is asked to say one thing he or she is thankful for. Extemporaneous and impromptu speeches are also categories in speech competitions. The participants don't know the subject until the contest starts. They are judged on how well they can converse about a subject without prior preparation. These competitions, though not always greatly publicized, are compelling to watch.

Inspirational

Sometimes the right words can completely change your mood. What a wonderful gift to be able to inspire with speech! Professional inspirational speech-givers include ministers and motivational speakers. You might object: "But nobody's going to hire me to preach or deliver a motivational address, so why would I need to know anything about inspirational speaking?" Ah, dear friend, that's where you're wrong—and why you're reading this book. Think about these situations: Your older sister has a baby, and at the shower she scans the room looking for someone who can say a few words to celebrate the happy occasion. At a worship service, a young person (that would be you) is asked to lead a prayer. The team lost the big championship game and Coach wants someone to say something to cheer everyone up. The person who can speak the words that express the joy that everyone feels, bring comfort, or that encourage hope—that person is a special one indeed.

No matter what type of speech you are giving, there are basic elements that apply to each form. A speaker needs to be able to organize ideas, talk in a way that is easy to understand, and have confidence. This last quality is important. You won't be able to speak a word if you can't overcome your stage fright. And just how do you do that? I'm glad you asked, because I'm about to show you why stage fright is your friend.

CHAPTER 2

Stage Fright Is Your Friend

"There are two kinds of fears: rational and irrational—or, in simpler terms, fears that make sense and fears that don't."
—*Lemony Snicket*

What you think is fear is actually something wonderful—and something necessary. Let me explain.

When I was a kid, I loved performing. Acting in plays, reciting at programs, giving speeches—I liked the stage. People would ask me if I felt stage fright. I always said no. I never did (okay, almost never). It was years before I truly realized what they meant.

Often, before I had to make a speech, I felt a funny feeling in my chest. It was like a big ball of energy roiling inside me, just behind my rib cage. It felt impossible to control or contain. I learned that I could handle it better by being quiet in the minutes before it was time to speak. Yes, it was somewhat unsettling, but not scary. In fact, I learned to welcome that fiery, churning sensation. I discovered that the bigger and more uncomfortable that feeling was, the better I tended to do once I was on stage. That nervous energy was the powerful force I needed to do the work of performance. It's the energy that helps me to speak loudly enough so that the people in the cheap seats in the back of the room can hear me. It's the extra spark that inspires me to add a gesture or a flourish as I'm talking. It's the energy that gives me the courage to "give attitude" or to throw in a dramatic movement. It's what gives me presence on stage. It's an important and positive thing.

Chances are you experience something similar when it's your turn to speak. Butterflies in your stomach. A trickle of perspiration snaking down your neck. A trembly feeling in your bones. Whatever you call it, that's not fear. That's your body revving up for action. Don't call it fear. Call it *power*.

HOW TO MANAGE NERVOUSNESS

Okay, so you've got all this power raring to go! It's bound to make you feel a bit unsteady if you don't know how to harness it. Here are some ways to channel your nerves into public speaking prowess.

Think Excitement

Have you ever been eager to get started on a favorite activity? Let's say your friend has promised to take you to a new theme park. You feel a certain anticipation, an enthusiasm, an

I-can't-wait-to-get-to-it sensation. Are you scared? No. You would describe what you feel as excitement and you embrace that excited feeling.

Think about riding a bike. A bicycle can move you faster and further than walking on two flat feet. On a bicycle, you can almost feel like you're flying—the wind whipping past you, the air flowing through your hair. It's exhilarating, isn't it?

But you know that riding a bike can be risky. You could fall off and scrape your knee, break your leg, or worse. You were probably worried about falling down and hurting yourself when you first learned to ride a two-wheeler. But what felt like fear when you were new to the experience became excitement once you learned how to do it. A fearful feeling is a normal thing to experience when trying something new. But that feeling could just as easily be described as excitement. If you feel scared when you think about public speaking, redefine that feeling. Stage fright? *Nah*. Stage *excitement*.

Think Opportunity

Are you afraid of getting a bonus on your summer job? Would it scare you to get a day off from school? Of course not. These events would thrill you. You would take delight in the opportunities these circumstances would afford you. Public speaking is like hitting the jackpot or celebrating a holiday. When you become comfortable speaking, you get to be the VIP in the room, lead the poetry slam team to victory, persuade Mom or Dad to upgrade your phone, or impress the cutie you admire. Skillful speaking opens doors.

Think Strong

That nervous feeling that you fear will be your undoing is going to be your strength. And that's not just mental acrobatics to twist your mind around. It's true. Overcoming something difficult is a grand way to empower yourself. Do you know why superheroes are heroes? Because they face the bad guys and prevail. You don't have to face any villains or fight with your fists. You just need to face a scary feeling and push through it. Tell yourself that you can do it. *I can do it! I can do it!* Tell yourself you're good. *I'm gonna be good! I am good!*

Positive thinking leads to positive energy, which leads to positive results. Ask a friend to be a cheerleader. Pick someone who will say to you: *You can do it, you're gonna be good!* If you're too shy to ask somebody to do that, then say it aloud so that you can hear it. Write it down and tape it to the wall. Remind yourself that people—just like you—give speeches every day and live to talk about it.

Think Funny

Speaking is fun. You may not believe me yet, but I'm saying it again it because it truly is. You get to stand in front of everyone and command attention. You can act out on stage in ways that would get you in trouble if you did it in the classroom. You can be loud, you can be silly, you can be oh-so-dramatic. You become, for that moment, a star.

With all this attention zooming in on you, how do you keep from freaking out? Speakers from the beginning of time have pictured the audience in their underwear to help them stay cool. Or imagine that all of them have cauliflower heads. The image will make them seem so ridiculous you'll be laughing so hard inside, you won't have energy enough to be scared. A silly image will remind you not to take it all so seriously. The audience is there to enjoy you. You're there to enjoy you, too. So enjoy yourself.

Think Ahead

One of the good things about fear is it spurs you to prepare. Because you are aware of some of the things that could go wrong, you can take steps to head them off. Afraid of forgetting what to say? Then rehearse your remarks. Afraid of looking stupid? Plan to wear an outfit you feel comfortable in. Afraid of getting a bad grade? Study.

When your fear is channeled, it becomes a positive activity. Don't fall into worry, which is repeatedly agonizing over the potential problems. If you let your fear lead you into action, then you won't panic about the situation. Action is an antidote to fear.

Preparation goes a long way toward building confidence and quelling nerves. Prep is the recipe and the remedy. When you have a plan, it readies you, and when you follow the plan, it steadies you. To be sure, not everything always goes to plan, but it's still a big help. (And there are ways to handle it when things veer off plan. More about that later.)

Find someone who is good at public speaking and who does it on a regular basis. Ask that person how he or she manages pre-speech jitters. Try some of those techniques to see which ones work for you.

Face the Fear and Do It Anyway

Do you know what *FEAR* stands for? Face Everyone And Recite. That's what you're about to do, Brave One. Are your knees knocking? No matter. It happens to the best of us.

So what, you're scared. Did you know that Abraham Lincoln had a fear of public speaking? Did you realize that Willard Scott, who used to be the *Today Show* weatherman, panicked every time just before he went on camera? He did the *Today Show* for 35 years and suffered anxiety attacks before going on-air most of that time. Singer Adele told *Rolling Stone* magazine she's scared of audiences and sometimes vomits before going onstage. Rihanna, Beyonce, Harry Styles—yep, they've all said that they've suffered performance anxiety. Lots of people get the jitters before they step up, but they face the fear, then suit up and show up anyway.

Besides, when you really think about it, what is there to be scared of? A flubbed phrase? A forgotten line? There are ways to cope with and correct that. (More about that in Chapter 9).

Nearly everyone in the audience is going to be pulling for you. Remember what I said earlier, that public speaking is a number one fear for many people? That means as soon as you step out on the platform, you've already won the admiration of most of the people seated before you. You're doing something they're too scared to attempt. They want you to succeed. They think you're a hero. They'll be considerate if you make a mistake. And they'll cheer for you when you're finished.

Now go out there and speak.

Try This

Your whole body runs on air. You can live a few weeks without food, and a few days without water. But only seconds without breathing and you're a goner. Breathing deeply does a body good. Try this breathing exercise to relax. Take a slow deep breath as you silently spell the word B-R-E-A-T-H-E. Then hold the breath inside as you think B-R-E-A-T-H-E again. Next, exhale slowly as you silently spell B-R-E-A-T-H-E. Repeat this several times or until you feel calmer.

CHAPTER 3
How to Get Started

"A blank page is God's way of showing you how hard it is to be God."

—*Anonymous*

<u>Monday.</u>

    TEACHER: Write a speech.

    YOU: Huh?

<u>Friday.</u>

    TEACHER: Have you written your speech?

    YOU: Um . . .

What happens if nothing happens when you begin work on your presentation? You've got nothing thinking, nothing saying, nothing doing. This syndrome is called *writer's block*, and there are ways to escape that block and move to a friendlier neighborhood. Being blocked is a common condition among people who are trying to create, but you can move beyond that mental stop sign and tap into a flow of ideas.

Here are some ideas for beating writer's block. Some of these things you can only do if you're at home. Some you can do in school. So I'll give you two versions of most of these techniques, depending on where you are when you get caught in a speechwriting traffic jam.

Take a Hike, Mike

How do you escape writer's block? Well, what would you do if you really wanted to get off the actual block where you live and go somewhere else? You'd walk away—or maybe skip or jump or run away. Doing something physical is one remedy. Movement is motivating, and stimulating other parts of your body in addition to your brain may be necessary. Perhaps you'll take ten minutes to jump rope, take a walk around the block, or do a few lay-ups on the backboard in your driveway.

Classroom Version

In your seat, stretch, twist, and make circles with your head. Ask to go to the bathroom; actually go, and come right back, but focus on your movements as you do so. Ball up some paper and walk to the wastepaper basket. Don't bump or trip up some other kid. Don't get carried away. You're just giving your body a chance to move a little before you get back to work.

Play a Tune, June

Music makes a wonderful counterpoint to too much thinking. If you're stuck, music could be a great ungluer. You can play it in your head or on a musical instrument. Give yourself over to your music library or the radio and listen to some of your favorite jams. Don't just listen, sing along. Or, sing without having anything to sing along to! Who knew singing karaoke could get your speech written?

Some say that music without words is best at stimulating the brain. You might try listening to some instrumental pieces, especially jazz and classical music. Bach, Beethoven, Dizzy Gillespie, and Miles Davis are some of the greats. Even if these musical genres and geniuses have never appealed to you before, you might try them on for size if your speechwriting is stuck.

Don't forget about making your own music by playing an instrument. Mom and Dad will be so happy that they don't have to nag you to practice! Shock them by picking up your guitar or going to the keyboard and playing for a while. After your musical vacation, come back to your paper and see what happens.

Classroom Version

Call up a favorite song or practice playing a musical piece and listen to it in your head. Do not turn your tabletop into a drum or start rapping. You're going to enjoy this musical performance only in your imagination. Silently.

Q & A with Jay

Wondering how to start? Do what I just did with this paragraph and pose some questions. Get a friend to interview you about the subject. Surely, you know somebody who would love to be Oprah for a day. They don't have to be an expert on astronomy or anatomy or ancestry or whatever your assignment may be. They just have to be willing to be a make-believe talk show host for a few minutes. Pay attention to the questions your friend asks, and write down your responses. Then use them to begin formulating your talk.

Classroom Version

Interview yourself! Make a list of questions about the topic and jot down the answers.

Make an Affirmation, Jason

Remind yourself that you are awesome. Take a look at the word *awesome*. The last two letters of the word shows you who the word applies to. So go to the mirror and tell yourself: "I am writing a great speech." Or affirm: "I can do this." Make up an affirmation of your own. Word it so that it is in the present. "I am a capable and awesome student" is more effective than "I will become a capable and awesome student."

Classroom Version

Write the affirmation down ten times. After ten times, if you still feel uncertain, write it down five more times. Write a message to yourself listing the positive things that will happen if you tackle this project. For example, "I will learn something new" could increase the likelihood of getting a good grade. "If I do it now" means I won't have to worry about it all week.

Blog Away, Renee

Have you ever tasted calamari? Does it sound like a dish that is exotic and tasty? It probably sounds more appetizing than if I said "How about trying some fried squid?" which is what calamari actually is. Sometimes, what you call a thing influences what you think about it.

In a similar way, instead of thinking that you have to write a report or present a paper, think about creating a blog. A blog is short, more fun to work on, and may make it easier to jump into the project. If you think of your talk as something you plan to share with friends over social media, that's less intimidating than thinking of it as A MAJOR ASSIGNMENT. That may make it easier to jump into it.

Classroom Version

Jot down a tweet-size summary of your topic. Then come back to this later and expand it into a speech.

Take a Pic, Vic

I'm a writer who loves writing and adores books, but sometimes even I get tired of the page and the computer screen. When I get "word blind," I have to look at pictures as an antidote. That is when I watch silly TV or go to the movies. The only book I'll look at is a picture book.

What's better than looking at still or motion pictures of things? Looking at the real thing itself. Go outside and look—really *see* the tree, the squiggle in the crack of the sidewalk, the gait of the man crossing the street. What color is the sky today? Is it really blue, or is it some other combination of colors? Let your eyes enjoy themselves. Then come back to your paper refreshed.

Classroom Version

Flip through the textbook that has the most pictures (probably your history or social studies book). Look around the classroom as if seeing it for the first time. Gaze out the window (but don't do it for so long that the teacher gets mad at you).

Time to Clean, Aileen

Clean up! Those odious words might turn you off enough to rush back to your computer to come up with something—anything—to avoid having to do chores. If so, this trick has done its job. But if you're still not inspired, go ahead and start picking up things, putting them away, and making things neat. Sometimes, outer order can lead to inner order. When your surroundings are orderly and uncluttered, you can compose your mind, making it easier to compose your speech.

Household chores are nowhere on my list of fun things to do. Yet, when I know I need to knuckle down and write, all of a sudden I get an itch to rush around the house and sweep floors or wash dishes or tidy up the bedroom. After a flurry of activity, I remind myself of the other work that has to get done, the work that I originally planned to do, and I go back to that blank sheet of paper. Maybe the cleaning helps to clean out the junk in my brain so that I can think clearly.

Classroom Version

Straighten your desk and/or your locker by going through your papers and throwing out anything you don't need anymore. Delete outdated files on your laptop or tablet. Delete old voice or text messages on your phone. Volunteer to help the teacher clean up the classroom.

Let's Play, José

Recreation centers. Recess. Video arcades. They were all created for playing. Just like taking vitamins and breathing oxygen, playing is good for you. Weekends. Comic books. Backyards. These are all ways to get a much-needed break from the regular routine. If you're not making progress on your speech work, maybe it's time to take a break. Don't spend the whole day looking at goofy videos of puppies or sending messages to your buddies. Take twenty minutes to distract yourself with an enjoyable activity. Then go back to work. Chances are you'll return refreshed after you've had some relaxation. When you break down the word *recreation* to *re-creation* you've got a clue as to its deeper meaning.

Classroom Version

Close your eyes and remember a fun time. Now, open your eyes so the teacher won't think you're asleep. But keep the memory of the fun time in your mind. Then try to work on your speech again.

Work by Not Working

Give yourself plenty of time to work on your speech. Working last minute, even if it's good, is an excessively stressful way to get something done. Besides, when you have some space in front of you before you sit down to that blank page, you'll have an extra asset working on your behalf.

You probably will not write your whole speech in one sitting. Work on it, turn your attention to another activity, then come back to it. Trying to compose the whole thing in one effort may not be the best way to prepare. Believe it or not, your brain will be secretly working on your remarks while you're eating dinner, filing your fingernails, and even sleeping. In fact, your subconscious mind will come up with ideas while you're *not* actively thinking about the presentation. Later, when you come back to your paper after not working on it, you will have better ideas to add to your talk. Be sure to give yourself plenty of advance time to work on your speech so that you can take advantage of the subconscious process to make your work richer.

During this period when your brain is unconsciously collecting ideas, you may want to consciously collect some ideas, too. If you hear a good turn of phrase or anecdote, remember it so that you can use it—and acknowledge the person who said it—in your speech. As time goes on, you'll have saved up a lot of stories and quotes for use in future speeches.

Try This

Collect (or even memorize) some quotations that you like so you can have them at hand to include in a speech.

CHAPTER 4
Organizing Your Speech

"It's better to look ahead and prepare than to look back and regret."

—*Jackie Joyner-Kersee*

Some people say that good things come in threes. Our meals come in threes: breakfast, lunch, and dinner. Summer vacation is June, July, and August. A human being has a body, a mind, and a spirit. Time is divided into the past, the present, and the future. The sky contains the sun, the moon, and the stars.

A speech is organized in the same way. There's a beginning, a middle, and an end, or to be more precise, an introduction, a body, and a conclusion. If you're preparing a speech, you need to think about how to organize each part. A lot of people start the speech writing process with an outline. Others make a list of the things they want to be sure to say. Still others start by jotting down the things that are most interesting to them, then later organizing it into a logical order. (That's the way I like to do it. In fact, when I was in school, I could never prepare a talk or a report by first doing an outline. I always wrote the speech or the paper, first, *then* did the outline to satisfy the teacher.) There's no one right way to begin as long as you wind up with a good beginning, a solid middle, and a satisfying end.

Veteran speakers often say every speech is nothing more than this: Tell 'em what you're going to tell them. Tell them. Then tell 'em what you told them.

INTRODUCING THE INTRODUCTION

Here's your chance to grab the audience's attention. So start strong. Speak up. Stand where they can see you. Pause for a moment before you open your mouth to give the audience a chance to quiet down and become ready to receive you.

When you're writing a speech, your introduction is the place where you set your talk in motion. It's the time in the speech where you capture the audience's attention. That means you want to introduce the topic in a way that captivates people, stimulates them, and makes them want to hear more.

Variations on an Introduction—The Quotation

For example, if your topic is Shakespeare, don't start the talk by saying, "Ladies and gentlemen, I have a speech about William Shakespeare." *Snooze city.* What might be more interesting is to lead with a very brief passage from

Shakespeare, such as "Be not afraid of greatness. Some are born great. Some achieve greatness, and others have greatness thrust upon them," from his play *Twelfth Night*." Or toss out a Shakespearean insult or two: "Thou art like a toad; ugly and venomous," or "Thou beslubbering fool-born flap-dragon!" Or maybe you could spoof Shakespearean-style language, saying "Gadzooks! 'Tis time to learn about the life of a poet of old."

Variations on an Introduction—The Song

You've heard rap records that "sample" music from other artists. Sampling is taking a line or two from a well-known song and singing it as part of your piece. You can try that as an attention-getting opener. Sing just a short lyric—not the whole thing—from a song everybody's familiar with that ties in with your subject. For example, if you have to deliver an oral report on the Farm Workers Movement, the song that labor leaders often sang during protests, "We Shall Not Be Moved," might be memorable. You don't necessarily have to have a fine singing voice to pull this off. Just make sure you practice it before you do it!

Starting with a Startling Statement

A startling statement is pretty much what it sounds like. You say something that is surprising or unusual or makes someone go "*Hmmm . . .*" Let's go back to Mr. Shakespeare.

You may start off a talk about him by saying, "Did you know Shakespeare *had* to get married? His bride was Anne Hathaway. He got her pregnant before they got married, which was a big no-no at that time. Plus, she was an older woman—she was 26 years old and he was only eighteen." Or how about this one: "William Shakespeare was born in 1564 on April 23. And when did he die? Fifty-two years later on *April 23.*" These are not the typical facts one hears about an august historical figure like William Shakespeare, and they are likely to perk up your listeners' ears.

If you can, paint a picture. Rather than say the Washington Monument is an obelisk, a style of architecture found long ago in Egypt, you might say, "Picture the Washington Monument in *red* and only one-eighth as tall. That image is an obelisk from ancient Egypt, and that's what inspired the design of the Washington Monument."

Jokes

Seasoned speakers often start speeches with a joke. That's okay if the joke or humorous story is related to the topic at hand. *And if it's funny.* Nothing's worse than a flat, unfunny joke. Unless you're good, leave the joke telling to the comedians. And if you do tell jokes, be sure they're not offensive. Don't use jokes that ridicule the opposite sex, ethnic groups, or people with disabilities. It's okay to poke fun at yourself—and maybe teachers (but don't get carried away!). A joke can be a friendly way to kick off a talk and help everyone to feel relaxed and open to the rest of the presentation.

BODY

The body of the speech is the meat of the sandwich. This is where you flesh out the information. This comprises the bulk of what you have to say, whether your topic is about scoring in soccer, the history of glue, or how to make pancakes.

Don't get overwhelmed by the fact that this is the largest and longest part of your speech. This is the place where you'll enjoy yourself the most. Here is where you contribute your knowledge, make your point, show off your skill. How do you make that happen?

Include both important facts and colorful details. The important points are the things your listeners most need to know, and the colorful examples are the things that will stick with them and help them remember the important facts. If, for instance, you are delivering a speech about teenage pregnancy, you'd probably want to mention the statistics about the numbers of teens giving birth, how that compares to previous years, or the names of programs that assist young parents. But for more colorful detail, you might also want to describe a typical teen mother (without using her real name) and some of the problems and challenges she faces, and how she feels about them. Using a description based on a real person helps the members of the audience put a face to the facts, and helps them better visualize the information you're giving them. Remember that old saying,

"A picture is worth a thousand words"? When you can create pictures with your words, your speech becomes a thousand times stronger.

The Story within the Story—Anecdotes

Using an anecdote (that's a short, usually amusing, story) that illustrates a key idea about your topic also makes for an engaging speech. Let's say you're doing a report on fashion designer Vera Wang. You'll mention where she trained (University of Paris, Sarah Lawrence College) and some of the places she worked before opening her own business (*Vogue*, Ralph Lauren). But it would be intriguing to tell a story about her time as a competitive figure skater and how that experience influenced her later career.

You may think anecdotes can only be applied in discussions of celebrities and can't work with speeches about ordinary folks or ordinary topics. Not so. Suppose you're writing a paper on the history of sound technology. Yes, you'll have to talk about how radio waves were sent via wires in the early days and how music was initially transmitted on a piece of tinfoil wrapped around a tube with grooves in it. You'll mention people like Thomas Edison, Alexander Graham Bell, and Guglielmo Marconi. But when you talk about the development of the telephone, you may interview your aunt and ask her to tell you about using a rotary phone and include that story in your report. Or maybe you can talk about the time you happened upon the old record player or cassette player in the closet at home and what your impressions were of this older sound technology. Adding stories always adds interest.

Rhetorical Questions

A rhetorical question is a question one asks without expecting an answer. Its purpose is to make the hearer think. Rhetorical questions are useful both in the beginning of a speech or in its body. These questions stimulate listeners to reflect more deeply about the subject at hand. Instead of stating that Bill Gates, the founder of Microsoft®, left Harvard to start his own company, you may pose the thought this way: "What if Bill Gates had decided to stay in school instead of dropping out to start his computer software company? Would someone else have come up with similar ideas, or would the digital world have taken a much different path?"

Asking your audience to imagine how things could have happened another way or to consider other outcomes both focuses their attention and widens their understanding. In a persuasive speech, the rhetorical question is especially effective. It helps do your work for you because it causes more reflection and hopefully more appreciation of your viewpoint by the listener. After posing a rhetorical question, pause. That will allow the thought to sink in.

Mark One, Mark Two . . .

It's a good idea to give your listeners markers, to let them know how your remarks are organized. If you begin by saying, "There are four ways to improve study habits," or "I will be discussing three aspects of the life of Harriet Tubman: her life as a slave, her life on the Underground Railroad, and her role during the Civil War," you give your listeners a way to know how you've ordered your thoughts, how long the speech will be, and where you are in the process. Markers are also ways to help you transition from one idea to the next. If you're discussing the history of Apple computers and you have divided the talk into two sections, it's easy to move smoothly from one section to the next. "We've been talking about how Apple Computers got started. Now we will look at how things have changed since its founder, Steve Jobs, died."

The ideal number of points to make is three. Generally, it's best not to have more than five points to make. More than that and your audience isn't likely to keep track of them all. You don't want them to stop listening before you've stopped talking.

Try This

Pay close attention to the next few speeches you hear. Can you identify the markers the speaker uses to transition from one section of the speech to the next? Is there a sentence or story the speaker used that stands out in your memory?

I won't lie to you, it does take focus and effort to compose the speech's body. Your thoughts probably won't line up in ABC order. As you find more information to include, you'll

43

have to revise. Come to the page knowing that reworking and rethinking the paper is an unavoidable part of the process. Then once you've finished the middle, you can begin to finish the end of your speech.

Conclusion

The conclusion of your speech is your opportunity to drive home the message. You tie up all the loose ends and make your final point. Summarize the key ideas. This means you'll briefly restate significant ideas you want your audience to hold onto. For example, in a speech where you've cautioned classmates about Internet safety, you might sum things up by repeating three tips to protect yourself. "Remember these three things to stay safe while surfing: Don't give out personal information such as your name, address, phone number, or picture. Don't respond to anyone who is being rude or bullying. And don't use a credit or debit card online before checking with your parents."

You may want the audience to do something as a result of hearing your remarks. In your conclusion, you can put out a call to action: "I want everyone to vote for Monica Vasquez for student council president" or "It's your responsibility— don't let friends drive drunk." You may want to leave the audience with something to reflect upon. In that case, you may conclude with a thought-provoking question: "How would you handle the same situation?" or "If you don't do it, who will?"

Some of the same things that work at the start of a

speech are also effective as a closing, like a song or a quote. The last thing you say may well be the main thing they remember, so make sure it's strong.

When you get to the end of a TV show, the credits begin to roll. When you get to end of movie, the words *The End* appear on the screen. In many books, you know the story is over because the last page is a blank page—nothing more to read here! The verbal way to signal the end of your speech is to have a moment of silence after your last sentence, then saying "Thank you."

CHAPTER 5

Polishing Your Speech

> "They did a little school survey asking children which they preferred and why—television or radio. And there was this 7-year-old boy who said he preferred radio 'because the pictures were better.'"
>
> — *Alistair Cooke*

Have you ever seen a TV show? Have you ever watched a YouTube video? Of course you have. It's likely that part of what captured your attention were the moving pictures. But did you know you can create pictures that move your listeners without lights and cameras? The way to polish up your speech once you've gotten the basics down on paper is to use literary devices. Combining words plus word images gives your speech both substance and splash. Literary devices are the special effects of written and spoken language. They amp up the interest and intensity of your presentation. Let's look at some techniques that will make your speech deliver punch and display pizazz.

Strong Similes, Mighty Metaphors

The first technique is the simile. A simile is making a comparison using the words *like* or *as*. Similes equate two things to each other in order to make a stronger point. The comparison plays up a key characteristic of the idea under discussion. Common similes are *strong as an ox, proud as a peacock, tough as nails, sing like an angel,* and *swim like a fish.* But don't use these examples—no, no, no! These expressions have been spoken to death. Take time to come up with your own original similes for your speech.

Fresh Similes!

Fresh similes! Come and get your hot, fresh similes! Do this exercise to help you think up original comparisons. In each instance below, write down all the things that come to mind when you hear that word.

Example

Word: *Hot*

Things that are hot: fire, sun, Tabasco™ sauce, chili peppers, boiling water, steam kettle, a teacher scolding a troublemaker, 12:00 noon in the desert.

Word: *Strong*

Things that are strong: _____

_____

47

Word: *Cold*

Things that are cold: _____

_____

Word: *Sweet*

Things that are sweet: _____

_____

Now rewrite these sentences using similes to make them as fresh as a daisy—um, no, let me try again—as fresh as a crisp apple on an autumn day.

The August afternoon was as hot as _____

_____.

His muscles were strong like a _____

_____.

Her rejection of him was cold like a _____

_____.

The baby was as sweet as a _____

_____.

A second literary technique is the use of *metaphor*. A metaphor is also a comparison, but instead of saying one thing is *like* another, you state that something *is* another thing—it's a little more subtle, but can be more powerful, and can give your writing a bold and vivid flavor. You can see how saying "It's raining cats and dogs" conveys just how strong the downpour is rather than just saying "It's raining hard." Other popular examples: "The old computer is a dinosaur."

"Baby you're a firework." "America is a melting pot." "Time is money."

Find the Metaphor!

Musical lyrics often use a lot of metaphors. Think of three popular songs to which you know the words. For example, in the nursery rhyme "Row, Row, Row Your Boat," a metaphor appears in the last line: "Life is but a dream." Try to find metaphors in other songs you know and like. If it fits, you might even sample the line in your speech.

Song

"Love Is an Open Door" from the movie *Frozen*. Lyric: "Love is an open door."

Song: _____

Lyric: _____

_____

Song: _____

Lyric: _____

_____

Song: _____

Lyric: _____

_____

Fancy Phrases

Have you ever heard this statement? "Many are called, but few are chosen." I'm guessing you have. (In case you're wondering, it's found in the Bible, Matthew 22:14.) What about: "It was the best of times, it was the worst of times"? You may have said one of these quotes yourself, even if you didn't know where it came from. (That last one is from the book *A Tale of Two Cities* by Charles Dickens.) No one really knows where some familiar phrases came from, such as "Easy come, easy go," and "Like father, like son." Or you've probably repeated the catchphrase or jingle for a commercial for Coke® or Nike® or PlayStation® or some other popular product. The reason people repeat these quotes so often is because the sentences have a rhythm and configuration that make them remarkable. Let's look at ways you can create your own memorable phrases.

One way is a construction called *antithesis*. *Antithesis* is a fancy word for *opposite*. In speech writing, *antithesis* means putting two contrasting or opposite thoughts together. Some examples: "Say what you mean and mean what you say," which means be honest and forthright in what you tell people, or "You can fool all the people some of the time, and some of the people all the time, but you cannot fool all the people all the time," which suggests that you may be able to get away with deceiving folks on occasion, but eventually your lies will catch up with you. And how about, "To be or not to be, that is the question"? (I'll leave your English teacher to explain that one.) Lining up the contrasting ideas makes the thought behind them stand out.

Another literary technique is the use of parallel language. Parallel language is composing a sentence that has a symmetrical structure. Let me show you what I mean:

> They liked singing, acting, and dancing.
> They liked to sing, to act, and to dance.
> They liked singing, acting, and to dance.

The first and second sentences here use a parallel construction. The first sentence formulates the verbs with the -*ing* ending (that is, a gerund), whereas the second sentence uses the infinitive form of the verbs. The third sentence lacks parallel structure, because "to dance" is different in structure from "singing" and "acting." Sentences with a parallel structure flow a lot better when you read or speak them. After you've written the first draft of your speech, go through it to see where you can tighten up the arrangement of your words and improve the rhythm. With parallel language, the words are organized according to a pattern, and if the sentence breaks from the pattern at some point, those words have even more weight. Take a look at these sentences. Some are pretty straightforward and some play with parallel structure a bit:

> ". . . government of the people, by the people,
> for the people, shall not perish from the earth."

> "It's not what you know, it's who you know."

> "The needs of the many outweigh the needs
> of the few."

"Every day may not be good but there is good in every day."

"Things turn out best for the people who make the best of the way things turn out."

"What goes around comes around."

"One spirit, one team, one win."

You may notice that a particularly skillfully constructed sentence may include the use of both antithesis and parallelism: "The happiest people don't have the best of everything, but they make the best of everything," or "Speech is silver, but silence is gold." But of course, speech can be silver, gold, and platinum overlaid with pearls and coated with greenbacks if you apply all the ideas in this book to polish your public speaking!

A well-worded phrase is easy to remember and helps cement the ideas you present in the audience's minds. It's worth it to tinker with your sentences to see if you can craft a clever turn of phrase. And here's some good news—you don't always have to come up with the statement yourself. If someone else has come up with a clever quote, sometimes you can just build on their work.

Try This: Give It a Spin

Can you put a twist on these familiar quotes?
Take a look at the original, then see if you can add your own spin and generate a new thought on the sentence. Here's one I like:

Original: If at first you don't succeed, try, try, again.

Twist: If at first you don't succeed, you're not us.

Now your turn:

Original: Don't hate me because I'm beautiful.

Twist: Don't hate me because I'm _____

_____.

Original: Keep calm and carry on.

Twist: Keep calm and _____

_____.

Original: So many books, so little time.

Twist: So many _____,
so little time.

Original: Life is like a box of chocolates. You never know what you're going to get.

Twist: Life is like_____

_____. You never know what you're going to get.

Original: Laughter is the best medicine.

Twist:_____ is the best medicine.

Tell a Story

Which paragraph sounds more interesting?

Star Trek is a science fiction TV show that began in 1966. Although the original show only lasted three seasons, its popularity increased even after it went off the air. A lot of movies and other TV shows are based on the *Star Trek* theme. *Star Trek* continues to have a lot of fans.

or –

Star Trek began its existence quietly, like a snowflake dropping onto a blanket. But over time that snowfall became a cultural avalanche. This science fiction show inspired 13 feature films and six TV series, plus games, comics, and books. It introduced new catchphrases into everyday conversation, such as "Beam me up, Scotty" and "Live Long and Prosper." Fans of the show are called Trekkers or Trekkies, which is also the name of a documentary made about them.

Most people would find the second paragraph more interesting. Why is that? The second paragraph offers more detail and description. It also used some of the literary techniques we just learned about, such as simile and metaphor. Don't just throw out facts and figures in your speech. Illustrate what you mean. Make word paintings. Draw a picture for your listener's brain. How do you do that?

You don't need a paintbrush and watercolors. Just give an example. Make it specific rather than general. Explain how an individual has been affected by your subject. Or demonstrate how the topic plays out in everyday life.

Let's say your topic is STEM careers—careers in science, technology, engineering, and math. Rather than just reciting a list of jobs in each field and the dry statistics about those positions, discuss (or make up) a scenario about a typical scientist. Where did he or she go to school? Don't just state that engineers must attend college. Maybe you'll say that Robert attended Howard University's School of Engineering & Architecture, where he studied civil engineering. Now Robert works for the Federal Energy Regulatory Commission inspecting and evaluating dams. Tell students that they can land a similar job if they take courses in geology, calculus, and electrical circuitry. Making it personal, detailed, and descriptive enhances the information you share.

Strategically using some of these literary devices throughout your talk will spice it up. But don't be heavy-handed. A sprinkle of pepper gives a pop of flavor to a dish, whereas a pitcher of pepper poured over your plate would kill it. Use your literary devices like pepper—in moderation. Unique, well-thought-out phrases will have people walking away repeating your words and remembering your ideas.

Practice Makes Polish

After you've finished adding the special touches that literary flourishes can add, the other way to make sure your speech strong is to practice reading it so that you can hear how what you've written sounds. Repeat it numerous times so that you have a good feel and rhythm for the words and phrases. We'll talk more about practicing your speech in terms of presentation in the next chapter, but it's important to find a time and place to say the actual words out loud early on. It doesn't even matter if you have an actual person available to hear you or a device to record you. Thinking about the speech in your head is *not* the same as saying it out loud. Only when you speak it aloud will you be able to hear how you sound and pick out what phrases may need to change. Plus, you'll start to become more comfortable with the material. Practicing it aloud will be the final polish to make your speech pure perfection on paper. Now, we'll talk about how to bring it from your paper to your audience's ears.

CHAPTER 6
Delivering Your Speech

"Don't wish it were easier, wish you were better."
—Jim Rohn

O kay. You're in front of the class. Or you're behind the podium. There you are, up on stage. Is there a stampede of buffalo in the room? No, that's your heart hammering in your chest. And that fluttering sound you hear is your shaky hand jostling the paper your speech is written on. Don't worry. It's going to be fine. Those are just the signs that you're going to have the energy to deliver.

May the Force Be with You

Remember how I described that big cloud of power churning in my chest back in Chapter 2? That churning cloud or nervous tension is a friendly thrust. It's power, but you have to harness it. Have you ever heard of a steam engine? Steam is the mist of water droplets formed when water boils. Mist seems like such a wispy, wimpy entity. You can't hold it and you can barely see it. Yet steam can propel a multiton locomotive train more than a hundred miles per hour. The steam you blow off a hot cup of cocoa doesn't carry much force, but that head of steam building up inside your body before you deliver a speech is very forceful. You just need to know how to keep that forceful flow focused. Sometimes a little physical movement helps. Stretch or jog in place for a few steps. I know an actor who walks up and down the rows of the theater seats before the audience arrives. At the other extreme, I prefer to be very still and extremely quiet before it's time for me to speak. Breathing slowly, rhythmically, and deeply is always effective. As you give more speeches you will discover what helps you to ride the momentum and feel comfortable with that energy.

What I'm saying is this: you've got the power. Here's the polish to add to your power. Let's find out what to do to make you a brilliant speaker.

Look into My Eyes

It sounds intimidating, but eye contact is one of the most important things you can do when giving a speech. Look at the people in the audience. Yes, look at them. Eye contact helps the audience feel connected to you and more empathetic toward you. And it helps you to feel connected to them. It will remind you that you're talking to girls and boys like you, people who want to hear what you (yes, *you*) have to say, strangers who want to become your friends.

Looking at the audience also allows you to see if they

are following you. Do you see frowns, wrinkled brows, or tilted heads? Those are the ways humans use their faces to form question marks. Perhaps they can't hear you or don't understand what you mean. Do you see smiles, bodies leaning forward, and rapt expressions? That means they're hanging on your every word. You're doing great! You don't want to miss out on all that splendid feedback by staring down at your page, do you? Of course not!

Now, how exactly do you look at the people to whom you're speaking and read from your paper or laptop at the same time? This is how you do it. Look at a few words on the page, then glance up and say them. Then look back down to gather a few more words, then speak them to the group. Every so often, you need to stop reading to look at the people. It becomes easier to do with practice.

What if you absolutely, positively, cannot look people in their beady little eyes without getting freaked out? Here's a secret. Look at a spot above their eyes, around their foreheads. They'll never know the difference.

Be Loud, Speak Proud

At a church or in a temple—no. In a movie theater—no. At a library—no. During a math test—no. You shouldn't talk loudly in any of these settings. But when you're on stage, that's the time to be loud and speak proud. Being loud doesn't mean yelling. It means using your whole body as an instrument for your words. You're using more than just your throat. You're using your chest, belly, mouth, and emotions to amplify your voice. Project your voice. Don't shout, but speak from your diaphragm (that's the spot low in your chest but above your belly). Breathing deeply helps with projection. Sometimes people don't project because they are feeling afraid. Breathing deeply also helps to still your nerves. You want to make sure everyone can hear everything you say. Otherwise, what's the point in speaking?

Very, Vary

Every student has had to endure a lecture from a teacher who droned on and on. You know the one—he talks in a flat tone and his voice never changes. *Bo-ring!* Don't make that mistake. Vary the volume as you talk. End some sentences by lowering your voice. End others by going up. When you're practicing your speech ahead of time, experiment to see what works best. In some sections of your speech it may be good to pick up the pace. While reading other passages, slow it down a little. Read with expression.

This is especially important when you're reading something poetic or dramatic. Try to match the sound and feel of the emotions expressed in the words. For example, if you were reading the line "It was a dark and stormy night . . .," you might pitch your voice lower and slower. On the other hand, if you were saying "The man was chasing her through the alley, then around the corner and she ran, ran, ran, as hard as her legs could carry her, frantic to get away," you would probably speed up your speaking rhythm. Some sentences require you to pause. If you were to say, "Should all teenagers be allowed to vote?," you might pause to give the audience a moment to think about this idea before you go on to your next remark.

Try This

Read this sentence:

Let's eat honey.

Now, read this sentence:

Let's eat, honey.

How is the meaning of each sentence different based on where you pause or inflect your voice?

Looking Good

If your teacher came to school and decided to teach geometry wearing nothing but swimming trunks, what do you think would happen? You know what would happen— nobody would pay attention to the lesson that day. Not a soul would be able to focus on measuring the sides of an isosceles triangle or graphing points on a curve because everybody would be distracted by Teach's inappropriate outfit and hairy legs.

Don't let that happen to you. Dress to fit the occasion. As a rule of thumb, you can expect that the larger the gathering or the fancier the place, the more you have to dress up. Wear clothing that is neat, clean, and pressed. An outfit that is comfortable and well-fitting will allow you to give your full attention to your talk and not the fact that your shoes pinch or your belt is strangling your stomach. For an important or formal occasion, you may want to practice giving your speech in the clothes you plan to wear. That way you can be sure your clothes allow you ease of movement. They'll be one less thing to worry about when you step up to the mike.

Keep your papers flat on your desk or on the lectern. If you try to hold them they will tend to rattle, especially if you get nervous. Index cards can be handy to use for your notes. Because they are small, they are easy to handle, and because they are cardboard, they don't rattle. If you're using a presentation on a computer, don't direct all your attention at the screen. You still have to look at the audience and talk to *them*, not the computer and not to the wall.

Po-TAY-to or Po-TAH-to?

Make sure you know the correct way to say all the words in your presentation. Proper names, which may include words from foreign languages, should be checked, too. If you're not sure, look up how to pronounce a word in the dictionary. If you're still not sure, ask your teacher for the proper pronunciation. Hey—that's why dictionaries and teachers were invented. There are also websites online and apps that allow you to hear the preferred way to say a word. Here are a few sites:

www.howjsay.com
www.howtopronounce.com

Try This

Some words have two different ways of pronouncing them. Which way do you say the following words? Which way does the dictionary or the online site indicate as the preferred pronunciation?

aunt

Caribbean

either

neither

pajamas

pianist

Here is a list of words many people mispronounce. Check to be certain you know how to say them correctly:

athlete

February

forehead

genuine

guitar

library

naive

often

police

sherbet

suave

sword

theater

Take It Slow

People don't listen as fast as they can talk. As the speaker, you'll need to slow down so that your listeners can keep up. It's not unusual for people to talk at a rapid-fire rate to hurry-up-and-get-it-over-with when they have to step up and speak. I sympathize with your desire to rush but that's not the way to go. Go slow. I, too, have to make a deliberate effort to slow myself down. I tend to talk rapidly when I'm nervous. To remind myself, I write SLOW at various points in my notes. It takes time to hear and process oral communication. When reading aloud, your pace should be slower than the pace at which you read silently. You will need to practice this slower pace. Read your talk out loud, deliberately taking your time and using pauses to give emphasis to important ideas.

Try This

Find what your reading rate is by reading aloud a passage that is ten words long. Measure your rate by using a phone app, a clock, or watch with a second hand. If you want to be fancy, use a stop watch. Your rate is the total words divided by the number of minutes while delivering a speech. The rate of conversational speech is between 120 words per minute (wpm) to 200 wpm. Audio book readers or podcasters typically speak at a rate between 150–160 wpm. You should aim for that rate when at the podium.

Try This

Make your words or the spaces in between them bigger in your notes. Increase the size of the font or double space the sentences. See if the larger print or spacing reminds you to read and speak more slowly.

Posture

How you stand or sit affects your delivery, too. Good posture keeps your internal speaking equipment (vocal cords, throat, diaphragm, lungs) open and aligned. Be upright—that's correct, stand (or sit) up straight. But that doesn't mean you have to be stiff. Achieving good posture is finding that halfway mark between rigid and lax. Don't be a robot, but don't be a slouch, either.

What does good posture look like? Well, if you're standing, your weight is resting on your feet, your chest is out slightly, and your head is upright. Shoulder blades are relaxed down your back. You are looking forward but your head is tucked down just a touch. The most important thing is that you are not leaning or slouching and that your body is gently upright.

Practice

Pick one: a mirror, a recorder, a kind but honest human being. You will be using one of these (or perhaps all three) to get feedback on your speech before you give it. Try your speech on for size several times before you have to do it for real. Believe me, this will go a long way toward preventing embarrassing moments. During the first few rehearsals, you're learning the content. In the following rounds of practice (and yes, the word *round* has an *s* on it), you're to become free and easy with the material and find ways to embellish it. Plenty of practice will make the speech more entertaining for the audience and more enjoyable for you. Say your speech a few times *out loud, please*—reading it to yourself doesn't count. You will be surprised to find some things that need tweaking that you overlooked before.

Watching yourself say your speech in the mirror will help you to see exactly what the audience sees. (*Now* will you comb your hair?!) Speaking into the recorder gives you the opportunity to hear and play back the presentation so that you can revise and refine it. And a kind but honest human being can give you feedback on what worked and what didn't. When you pick a fellow human being to critique your talk, choose someone who will be truthful and will tell you what you need to fix but who will tell it to you gently.

Don't complain about any of the things that need fixing. Fix them and be glad you didn't make these mistakes in front of a large crowd. Don't complain about having to practice. Practicing is what's going to make your speech sparkle and shine. Practice gives you power!

Forget to Memorize

Don't try to memorize your entire speech. Don't do that to yourself or to your audience. It's hard to do and usually not effective, because memorized speeches sound stiff and monotonous. Your energy gets sapped as you try to recall every single little word, and you wind up with no spirit in your delivery. Memorization is typically only necessary if you're acting in a play or you are reciting a poem or a piece of literature. If you have practiced your speech several times (you have, haven't you?), then you should be familiar enough with the material to be able to talk from your notes without having every single item written out or committed to memory.

Don't think of your speech as a passage you have to recite line for line and word for word. Think of it as a conversation. You're having a conversation with ten or twenty or fifty people, one at a time, even though you're the only one talking. Think personal, and your delivery will have a relaxed tone that will put everyone in the room at ease, including you. Think friendly, and you'll exude a congenial air that will have everyone drawn to you like hungry kids running after an ice cream truck.

FAQ

Why do people fall in love? What is the meaning of the universe? When will the world come to an end? These are questions that can't be answered. However, you will probably be asked questions, and your audience will expect you to come up with some answers. You will know the answers to their questions. Why? Because you will already have guessed what the questions are likely to be.

Have you ever gone to a website that has a section called

FAQ? FAQ stands for Frequently Asked Questions and it's a list of the most common queries that the website writer expects folks to pose. You're going to do the same thing: anticipate the questions your audience will most likely ask and look up those answers. Maybe you already know the answers from the reading and studying you had to do to write your speech.

Decide in advance how you want to be questioned. Do you mind if people ask you questions as you are delivering your talk? Or do you prefer to have them hold all questions till the end? Whichever way you do it, it's good to tell them early in the talk how you'd like to handle that. If you are in a large space and audience members don't have a microphone, it's good for you to repeat the questioner's remark so that everyone in the room can hear what was asked before you respond to the question.

And if you don't know the answer to a question, it's okay to say, "I don't know." If it's appropriate, you can offer to find out and contact the person later to give them more information. Some people mistakenly think that to admit you don't know makes you look bad, but what will make you look bad is to give out wrong information in an effort to appear smart. You will get found out. Maybe not while the speech is ongoing, but people will discover your inaccuracy, or worse, your dishonesty. State what you do know. Admit what you don't know. Tell the truth.

———

Start on Time, End on Time

Were you assigned to present a five-minute report? Stick to five minutes. Were you asked to start at 10:30 a.m.? Begin your talk at half-past ten. Being prompt makes a good impression. It shows you are prepared and respectful of the people who are there to hear you. Ending on time keeps your listeners happy, too. As delightful as you are, listening to you is not the only thing that anyone wants to do today. If you are being graded on your presentation, it will help your score if you can judge time accurately and stick to the agreed-upon schedule. Of course, there are times when the program gets off to a slow start, the person who was supposed to go first gets shuffled to third place, or there's a fire drill and the whole timetable gets thrown off. But to the best of your ability, try to start on time and end on time. It makes life simpler for everybody, including you.

Try This

See if you can time yourself to talk for exactly sixty seconds without looking at the clock. Choose an open-ended topic. Here are a few topics, or you can choose your own:

- Recount the things you learned in your favorite teacher's class.

- Describe each of the four seasons.

- Talk about an entertaining video you've watched.

69

- Explain why a famous person's work is so important.

Try the same exercise again, but next time, time yourself for five minutes. Then try to do it for ten minutes!

CHAPTER 7
Dramatic Reading

> "The whole essence of learning lines is to forget them
> so you can make them sound like you thought of them
> that instant."
>
> —Glenda Jackson

Does your mother ever get on your nerves? When I was a kid, mine used to wear me out with her complaints about my behavior—and sometimes, she still does. (Mommy, if you're reading this . . . I love you!) That's why I immediately loved Elias—better known as 'Lias—from the first moment I was introduced to him. His mother was fussing at him because he couldn't get up and get going as quickly as she thought he ought to. *Hurry up and get out of bed. Comb your hair. Wash up, and you'd better not splatter any water.* Boy, have I heard the same things. Although it annoyed me when I heard it from my own mother, it was hilarious when I heard 'Lias's mother harassing him.

I met 'Lias at a church program many years ago when

I was in elementary school. Someone recited the poem "In the Morning" by Paul Lawrence Dunbar about a little boy whose mother is trying to wake him up and get him ready for the day. The reader performed the poem with such zest and enthusiasm that I could readily picture that mischievous, sleepy-headed boy, 'Lias! And all these years later I still feel the pleasure I took in hearing the poem recited. Wouldn't you like to have that effect on someone?

Bringing words to life is the art of dramatic reading. Dramatic reading, also sometimes described as oral interpretation, is the reading aloud of a piece of literature with expression. I love it when someone steps on stage and pours himself into a poem or transforms herself into the character in a monologue. When that happens, something delights me deep down in my soul.

I watch plenty of TV, spend more time online than I should, and enjoy a Hollywood movie every once in a while, but there's something about being in the room with a person who is not just telling a story, but inhabiting the story, that is transformational. It's like the boy who said he liked radio more than television "because the pictures are better." So what is it that performers do to make words transfigure into pictures without using color, paint, or a camera?

A good performer uses all the tools for delivering a speech that we discussed before, things like projecting the voice, vocal variation, pronunciation, and practice. But there are some other techniques, unique to dramatic reading, that we should discuss.

A Choice Voice

Your primary tool, of course, is your voice. Inflection, articulation, tempo, and tone will help you to carry the message. Even more than in a straightforward speech, vocal tone and variety are crucial. Inflection refers to how you moderate your voice: raising the pitch of your voice at the end of a question, or deepening your voice when stating something serious. Think about how music influences feelings. If you were a conductor scoring music for a symphony about war, you might use the thundering sound of drums to mimic the stomp of men marching to battle. If you were a choreographer and you wanted music to accompany a dance about flying, you might choose harp music, because it sounds light and airy, or the flute, because it's a wind instrument with a breezy character to it.

Articulation refers to the way in which your words are enunciated. When the author of your dramatic piece wrote it, he or she likely spent a *lot* of time choosing the words. You honor their work and give pleasure to the listeners by reciting these words with clarity and exuberance. It's like each word is a diamond you hold up to the light to best show off its sparkle.

These lines from "Song of the Witches" in the play *Macbeth* by William Shakespeare make music without need for a musical instrument through the rhyme and repetition of the sounds that end the words and those within the words. Clear, distinct, and energetic pronunciation makes for enjoyment on the part of both the speaker and the listener.

Double, double toil and trouble;
Fire burn and caldron bubble.
Fillet of a fenny snake,
In the caldron boil and bake;
Eye of newt and toe of frog,
Wool of bat and tongue of dog,
Adder's fork and blind-worm's sting,
Lizard's leg and howlet's wing,
For a charm of powerful trouble,
Like a hell-broth boil and bubble.

Nuanced articulation helps to make this next poem come alive. "Weather" is a traditional poem, meaning it's old and the writer is anonymous. (Isn't it amazing how clever and prolific the writer Anonymous is?) Being able to speak the words *weather* and *whether* in order to make the meaning clear makes this an amusing piece to recite.

Weather

Whether the weather be fine,
Or whether the weather be not,
Whether the weather be cold,
Or whether the weather be hot,
We'll weather the weather
Whatever the weather,
Whether we like it or not!

When you are reading a poem that is upbeat and humorous, your voice needs to sound bright and clear, and the rhythm of your speech up-tempo. If the story you are recounting has a section that is deep and philosophical, your tone should be thoughtful and measured.

Try This

Have you ever read *A Christmas Carol* by Charles Dickens? It's the story of Ebenezer Scrooge, a hard-hearted miser who loves money and hates nearly everything else. Take a look at this excerpt. Recite Scrooge's lines and his amiable nephew's lines in a way that clearly shows the contrast in the two men's personalities. For example, do you imagine that Scrooge would speak quickly or in long, considered sentences? Is his voice high or low? How can you say "Merry Christmas" the way his nephew would, where you can "hear" the smile in his voice?

"A merry Christmas, uncle! God save you!" cried a cheerful voice. It was the voice of Scrooge's nephew, who came upon him so quickly that this was the first intimation he had of his approach.

"Bah!" said Scrooge. "Humbug!"

He had so heated himself with rapid walking in the fog and frost, this nephew of Scrooge's, that he was all in a glow; his face was ruddy and handsome; his eyes sparkled, and his breath smoked again.

"Christmas a humbug, uncle!" said Scrooge's nephew. "You don't mean that, I am sure?"

"I do," said Scrooge. "Merry Christmas! What right have you to be merry? What reason have you to be merry? You're poor enough."

"Come, then," returned the nephew gaily. "What right have you to be dismal? What reason have you to be morose? You're rich enough."

Scrooge, having no better answer ready on the spur of the moment, said, "Bah!" again; and followed it up with "Humbug!"

Punctuate important points in the message with a beat of silence. You may pause for silence before an important line to signal to the audience that they should pay attention to what is about to follow. Or you may pause after the line so that they have time to let those words sink in. Which way do you need to do it? That will become clear once you practice it and see what feels right.

Try This

Watch a scary movie and note what kinds of music are used to highlight the scariest scenes.

Watch a romantic comedy and note what kinds of music are used in the scenes when the couple is happy and in love.

In any movie, pay attention when silence is used for more than two beats. How did the use of silence enhance the action?

Timing and Rhyming

Tempo is the rate at which you talk. You already know that your performance tempo needs to be slower than your conversational tempo. In general, that remains true for recitations, but depending on the particular portion of the reading you are reciting, that may need adapting. For a section of a monologue where the character is nervous and jumpy, you may want to talk in a tense and staccato style to vividly transmit that feeling. But even then, you must not speak so rapidly that your listeners can't keep up with what you're saying. With a rhyming poem, you need to be careful not to get enslaved by the sing-song nature of the rhyming pattern. Keep in mind that you're not *only* reciting the rhyme—all the words are there to tell a story. So as you talk, phrase the words to emphasize the meaning and not just the final words of each line.

The tone refers to the feeling quality of your words. Can the listener feel the happiness being described in the text by the way you are reading it? When the passage is something funny, is your timing tight—such that when the punch line comes, the audience gets it? Again, you can hone these skills by rehearsing. You may think that rehearsing a lot will kill the energy and spontaneity of your performance . . . but you would be wrong. The more you rehearse, the more the material seeps down deep inside of you and the easier it is to relax into it and make it more your own.

Try This

Watch some radio. Listening to fiction in an audio format may sound a bit tedious if you're used to getting all your stories screen-fed to you. As you listen, note how your imagination gets engaged through voice and sound effects. In cases where you're only listening to a sole storyteller, what techniques does he or she employ to keep your attention and to paint a picture of the scene in your mind? Here are some sites that specialize in radio drama to get you started:

This site sells dramas based on the popular—and extremely eerie—old TV series, *The Twilight Zone.* www.twilightzoneradio.com

Formerly known as *A Prairie Home Companion*, this was originally a radio broadcast on National Public Radio that includes short, humorous plays as part of the overall show. www.livefromhere.org

Radio Drama Revival is a site where up-to-date stories are told in the format of old-style radio plays. www.radiodramarevival.com

The Moth Radio Hour offers compelling contemporary stories told before a live audience. www.themoth.org/radio-hour

Memorization

Since you are reading a piece of literature written by someone else rather than a speech you have authored yourself, you'll need to be faithful to the written word. This means you may violate the rule I stated in the last chapter. You may want to memorize the work. Depending on the situation, you may have the work in hand so that you can read from the page during your performance. But if your assignment or competition requires you to memorize, then go ahead and start learning that story by heart. However, even if your goal is to memorize, your goal is not to merely call out the words accurately. The spirit you need to bring to the work is that of letting the message flow.

Body Language

When you speak, you aren't only conveying a message with your voice; your whole body is part of the message. Make the best use of it. Don't make the mistake of hunching over with your arms hanging down like a weeping willow because you're trying to look like you're sinking in sorrow or clasping your hands to chest to show hope. Although it requires a touch of acting, oral interpretation is more subtle. An occasional gesture, such as an arched eyebrow, or a faint smile on your lips while the eyes tell a different story—these more muted expressions may be more effective.

You already know the basics of what to do. The first part is to stand up straight, stand where people can see you, and own the space. The second part is to choose the gestures and movements that illustrate the mood and message of the piece you're performing. Even your nervous energy, which sometimes feels like a physical presence, can be used in service of the performance. I find that when I lean into all that energy coursing through my body, when I both mentally and physically accept that flow, it fuels my presentation. Confident physical behavior will translate into a confident performance.

How you look is part of the performance, too. Dramatic recitation doesn't require a costume, but you could add something to highlight the message. A hat, a scarf, or other garment or prop can be used, if appropriate. What makes it appropriate? The object must enhance what you're saying rather than becoming the main focus of the piece. Dressing all in black always works. It's the universally accepted uniform for dramatic presentations.

E-motion

The most critical aspect of reading a piece of literature is probably the ability to mirror the emotional truth of the piece. Are you reading a monologue about a teen who is struggling with the choice between right and wrong? Then you'll want to have a tinge of tension in your body language. Are you reciting an introspective piece? Then the audience will expect your demeanor to show some reserve. Someone once told me that emotion stands for *energy in motion*. Your challenge is to channel the emotion of the written word and express it through the spoken word.

How do we express these nuances? I think a first step is to think about what the author of the work is trying to say. Then ask yourself how it made you feel. Name the feelings and don't be surprised if some of them are opposites. Life is tricky. Oftentimes a sad situation also has a sweetness to it and a zany story has a sharp-edged truth hidden inside.

When you interpret a piece of literature you take on a stirring venture. You're doing more than being a rote report-reader. You become a magical message-maker.

CHAPTER 8
Could You Say a Few Words? Speaking Off the Cuff

"A proverb is the horse of conversation; when the conversation lags, a proverb will revive it."

—*Yoruba proverb*

If Mrs. Kim tells the class that everyone has to give an oral report on Friday during third period, then you know you have until third period on Friday to prepare your oral report. If you know that Youth Day is the second Sunday of next month and Pastor says you are the one chosen to be the MC, then you know that you will need to be ready next month on the second Sunday to MC at church. In these situations, you have time to pull your act together.

But how do you prepare for a speech you don't know you have to give until five minutes before you give it? What do you do when someone points a finger at you and says, "Come on up and say a few words!"? I have a few suggestions to help you come up with something intelligent—perhaps even inspiring—to say.

In speech and debate competitions, there is an event known as impromptu speaking. In this contest, someone writes a topic on a slip of paper and gives it to the contestant. The speaker is given seven minutes total to both prepare *and* deliver a speech on that topic. How can you make up an entire speech in such a small sliver of time? The answer is you're going to be doing the same things you do with a more formal talk. You'll have an introduction; one, two or three points; and a conclusion. It'll just be a lot more succinct.

Most of your impromptu speeches won't be contests. You'll be doing it as part of your regular, everyday life. Let's say it's the family reunion and everyone is at the dinner table. It's been fun catching up with people you haven't seen in years and making friends with cousins you didn't know you had. This will be the last time you will all see each other for at least another year. A few of the adults stand up and say a few words and although you're trying to hide behind a bowl of potato chips, Uncle Ned spots you and says, "Let's hear from one of the young folks!" Delivering a speech was the last thing on your mind; you were wondering if you should go for the ice cream or the pecan pie for dessert. What do you say?

The first thing you can say is a statement of the occasion. Give the reason why these people are here in *this* place and at *this* time. "We're gathered here today for the family reunion." "This is a major milestone for our school." "A graduation is a big step forward." Stating the occasion is a unifying move. It focuses peoples' thoughts on the purpose of the gathering. And it buys you a few moments to gather your thoughts.

Then you can use a sentence or two to express the mood. You want to say something that reflects the feeling in the room. "Everyone is happy that Julio is graduating." "What a beautiful time we're having today!" Even if it's a sad occasion, there is still a positive feeling you can express: "We didn't win but we sure worked hard." "He's no longer with us but we all loved Mr. Washington."

Now it's time to make some brief points. In the family reunion example, you may decide to point out how dedicated various people are to the family. "It's good that the Joneses came here all the way from Alabama—that shows how committed they are to being with family. And Aunt Lil has been in the kitchen all day—that's her way of showing love for all of us." You may offer some words of encouragement. Tell the graduate how proud everyone is of him. Congratulate the birthday girl. Let the team know that although things didn't go their way this time, there will be another chance. Or you may need to issue a call to action. That means there is something people need to do after the occasion is over: "Let's not wait till next year to raise money, let's plan to get together next month." "We learned a valuable lesson which we will use at Monday's meeting." Maybe someone needs to be thanked—or several someones do. However, that can be tricky if you're naming names because it's so easy to leave someone's name out by mistake (especially when you're called to speak off the cuff). It's usually safer to thank people in groups, saying something like, "I appreciate all the hard work Mr. Contee's class did," or "We thank the leaders of the committee for staying late after school."

Finally, you'll want to give a conclusion. Here are three ideas for concluding. One, you can close with a restatement of the occasion. Two, highlight and summarize the emotions everyone is feeling in different words. A third idea is to recite a quotation or a proverb as a tidy way to wrap things up.

It may help you in future impromptu talks to memorize a couple of favorite sayings or short poems to have on hand. With quotations, someone else has already done the work of crafting insights into a clever or deep or comical message. Here are some to try on for size:

For Happy Occasions

"This is the day that the Lord has made; let us rejoice and be glad in it."
—*Psalms 118:24*

"Whoever is happy will make others happy, too."
—*Anne Frank*

"Be happy. It's one way of being wise."
—*Colette*

"Whatever God gives you, enjoy!"
—*Lailah Gifty Akita*

For Overcoming Difficulty

"A setback is a setup for a comeback."
—*Willie Jolley*

"Once you choose hope, anything's possible."
—*Christopher Reeve*

"I'm not afraid of dying. I'm afraid of not trying."
—*Jay-Z*

"Don't think of all the misery but of the beauty that still remains."
—*Anne Frank*

"It's kind of fun to do the impossible."
—*Walt Disney*

To Celebrate Friends and Family

Make new friends, but keep the old;
One is silver and the other's gold.
—*Girl Scout song lyrics*

"The family is one of nature's masterpieces."
—*George Santayana*

"In every conceivable manner, the family is link to our past, bridge to our future.
—*Alex Haley*

"Family is not an important thing. It's everything."
—*Michael J. Fox*

"Walking with a friend in the dark is better than walking alone in the light."
—*Helen Keller*

To Inspire or Acknowledge Achievement

"It's easy to sit up and take notice. What is difficult is getting up and taking action."
—*Honore de Balzac*

"Nobody can do everything, but everybody can do something."
—*Gil Scott-Heron*

"A leader is one who knows the way, goes the way, and shows the way."
—*John C. Maxwell*

"Today a reader, tomorrow a leader."
—*Margaret Fuller*

Common Sense

"Who is wise? He who learns from all men."
—*The Talmud*

"The beautiful thing about learning is nobody can take it away from you."
—*B. B. King*

"Success doesn't lead to a positive attitude. A positive attitude leads to success."
—*Keith Boykin*

"Don't let what you can't do stop you from doing what you can do."
—*John Wooden*

"People who fight fire with fire usually end up with ashes."
—*Abigail Van Buren*

"People will forget what you said,
People will forget what you did,
But people will not forget how you made them feel."
—*Anonymous*

Try This

Every culture has proverbs that express practical and inspirational insights in their own unique way. I recommend learning proverbs from your own ethnic group as well as another. Repeating them will make you sound wise, too. Below are some common sayings. Can you match the meanings of these familiar sayings to proverbs from other cultures?

Common Sayings:

1. Sticks and stones may break my bones, but words will never hurt me. _____

2. Do unto others as you would have them do unto you._____

3. What goes around, comes around._____

4. Slow and steady wins the race._____

5. Nobody's perfect._____

6. Birds of a feather, flock together._____

7. Haste makes waste._____

8. Don't judge others until you've walked a mile in their shoes._____

9. Every cloud has a silver lining._____

10. Nothing lasts forever. _____

Proverbs:

A. "Even monkeys fall from trees."
—*Japanese*
B. "Clouds are not hurt by the barking of dogs."
—*Moroccan*
C. "Those who resemble, assemble."
—*French*
D. "It's fair that he who tried to steal yours, loses his."
—*El Salvadorian*
E. "Don't judge a man until you have walked two moons in his moccasins."
—*Cheyenne*

F. "Slow work—fine work."

—*Chinese*

G. "Haste is the mother of inaccuracy."

—*Native American*

H. "A sweet taste does not remain forever in the mouth."

—*Kenyan*

I. "Every tear has a smile behind it."

—*Persian*

J. "Say nothing about another that you wouldn't want to hear about yourself."

—*El Salvadorian*

Not every wise word comes from a book. Pay attention to some of the expressions your granddad or your favorite teacher or the lady next door often uses. A lot of the time, they have a turn of phrase that is cute and catchy—and astute as well. My grandmother used to say, "People are nothing but a bunch of walking habits." She would make that remark to warn me that repeating the same bad habits over and over again would lead to problems, but repeating good actions over and over again would lead to success.

Now, back to Uncle Ned putting you on the spot at the family reunion. Let's put together all the parts of the speech we talked about earlier.

> "It's great that everybody is here for the final dinner of our family reunion." (Statement of the occasion)

"I always feel good when I get to see the whole
family. And this year I got to meet new
cousins, which is really cool. And I can tell
all of you are feeling happy to be with each
other, too." (Expression of the mood)

"I wish I could see you guys more than once a
year. Let's exchange emails and Facebook
each other so we can keep in touch." (Call to
action)

"Like the famous actor Michael J. Fox said, 'Family
is not an important thing. It's everything.'"
(Close with a quotation)

See? That was quick and easy; nothing fancy but right on point. Now, take your seat and enjoy all the grown-ups praising you and talking about what an articulate young adult you are!

CHAPTER 9
Escaping the Yawn Zone, or How Not to Be Boring

"Perhaps the world's second worst crime is boredom; the first is being a bore."

—*Cecil Beaton*

No Yawning, Please

Sleep is a beautiful thing. Mattresses, feather pillows, down-filled quilts, lullabies, a golden watch swinging from a silver chain—these are marvelous things to make you fall asleep. Your speech should not be something to add to that list—you don't want it to be a sleeping pill! Lucky for you, there is a prescription for preparing a speech that won't be so boring it leads to snoring.

Don't chain yourself to a word-for-word written paper. When people read a speech word for word, the tendency is for them to fall into a monotone in which every word, phrase, and sentence is delivered in the same dead tone. They are more concerned with their attachment to the paper than their connection to the audience.

Let's look at ways to keep your speech engaging. There are some words and phrases I think you should avoid. They are dull and boring, dull and boring, and did I mention boring and dull? I dread when a student giving a book report begins, "This book is about . . ." Please, please, please, think of something else to say. Begin with a quote from the book, or a statement about something new you learned.

When Interesting Isn't Interesting

What sounds more interesting? Take a look at these pairs of sentences and decide which sentence paints a better word picture:

1-A. Observing the playful monkeys at the zoo was quite *interesting*.

1-B. Observing the playful monkeys at the zoo was quite *amusing*.

2-A. It's *interesting* how having money can make people want to be your friend.

2-B. It's *suspicious* how having money can make people want to be your friend.

3-A. It was *interesting* watching the acrobat flip and fly on the trapeze.

3-B. It was *thrilling* watching the acrobat flip and fly using the trapeze.

Interesting is a word often used to describe things. *Interesting* is an acceptable word. But if you use it more than once, it becomes flat. There are so many other words that probably describe what you mean more precisely. Instead of *interesting*, try substituting one of these: *appealing, engaging, fun, delicious, electrifying, noteworthy, curious, exciting, attractive.*

Really and *very* are also words that tend to be overused. Usually you can strike them out and your message will be just as clear. Similarly, *good* and *nice* are such bland terms. Sharp speakers avoid the vague and go for the vivid. If something truly is good or nice, can't you come up with an expression that does a smarter job of conveying just how good or nice it is? Is Sunil a nice boy, or do you mean to say he's helpful and friendly? When you say the dinner was good, might it be more on the money to describe it as spicy and well-seasoned?

Try This

Perk up these sentences by replacing the word interesting, good, or nice with more precise language:

1. Davon is an ~~interesting~~ _____
student; he has lived in several countries and can speak four languages.

2. The thing I find ~~interesting~~_____
about African history is the oral tradition of transmitting stories and information through the spoken word.

3. Spending a year living on a space station would be ~~interesting~~ _____.

4. Mr. Nakamura is a ~~good~~ _____ teacher.

5. OMG! The concert was so ~~good~~ _____!

6. That's a ~~nice~~ _____ car Nazia is driving.

7. Danny is a great date; he's a ~~good~~ _____ dancer and he always finds ~~nice~~ _____ restaurants for us to go to.

8. My speech is going to be ~~good~~ _____!

Vague vs. Vivid

Thesaurus sounds like an animal you'd find in Jurassic Park, but it's something a lot more practical: a speaker's friend. A thesaurus is a book of synonyms, which are words that have the same or similar meanings. It's useful when you want to replace a boring word with a more descriptive word.

Teacher Nancy Schwalb developed the following exercise to help her middle school slam poets write winning performance poetry. Come up with at least three vivid terms for each of the following vague words by using your thesaurus (or your own imagination).

Examples:

Vague	Vivid
building	*castle, shack, cathedral, firehouse, skyscraper*
person	*teacher, infant, senator, mailman, nurse, lost child*
nice	*helpful, mild-mannered, likable, pleasant*

Now you try a few:

car

_____

_____

ugly

_____

_____

happy

_____

_____

beautiful

_____

_____

sick

_____

_____

female

_____

_____

smart

_____

_____

book

_____

_____

The Short, the Long, the Varied

Vary your sentence structure. Don't begin every sentence with *I* or *the*. Make some sentences long and some sentences short. Some sentences might be only one word long. See? (That was a one-word sentence, in case you didn't notice.) When you rehearse your speech aloud, notice if your sentences all fall into the same pattern. If they do, change the words around. When you speak, the sound and rhythm of your words is almost as important as their meanings. Unlike a book or a computer, where everything is visual, when a person is presenting a message live, what you see plus what you hear all makes an impact. The spoken word has personality and verve that you can never experience on the page or the screen. Don't kill that personality by having your words be monotonous! Take full advantage of that when you choose the way you put your words together.

Try This

Read this sentence out loud:

Woman without her man, is nothing.

Now read this sentence out loud:

Woman—without her, man is nothing.

Note how the change in punctuation and the place where you put emphasis completely change the meaning of the sentence.

Just Say No to *Y'know*

Have you ever watched the news and seen this scenario? The reporter approaches Jane or John Doe and asks questions about the event that just took place:

Reporter: What happened during the hurricane?
Eyewitness: Y'know, it was like the storm caused the electricity to go out, y'know and lots of trees, y'know, fell down. Y'know, it was really scary, y'know?

Please say no to *y'know*. It doesn't sound intelligent. It takes away from the impression that you know what you're talking about. And you're going to make sure the people you're talking to know what you're talking about, so you don't have to keep saying *y'know*. It's an unconscious pattern, inserting expressions such as *y'know, um, and-uh,* or *er*. Other pet phrases I've heard people use include "You know what I mean?" "man," and "like." These expressions are verbal pauses to give someone a moment to think of the next thing to say. Thinking before you speak is a good thing. But if you need to pause, then simply pause and say nothing. Be silent. When you've gathered the next idea, then speak it.

The best way to break the *y'know* habit is to have a friend or teacher listen to you and point it out every time you say it. Once you become aware of what you're doing, you can stop.

Try This

Choose one of the following topics and talk for two to three minutes about it and record it. When you play it back, do you hear yourself using y'know or some other repetitive phrase?

Topics:

Give directions to get from your house to school, and name the landmarks along the way.

Describe the worst teacher you ever had.

Explain how to use a dictionary.

Tell the story of how you learned to ride a bicycle.

From Making Them Bored to Being Adored

How do you move from merely being unboring to being quite impressive? What can you do that will add more flash and flavor to your time on stage? Those speakers who are seen and heard and remembered have an added ingredient that makes them attractive. They have presence.

Look at the following passage:

wioeivne.wp[23jfie%#@milc/z.nmseo!@)
)9~43kesmpq93m.2b6395#*&.56qoitu3(!
nbvboespbk%$#7y=**camel***sdlsow;;lk8uu
cp@xx5-+==pt][%0s:::kesoapt%rr*""q2nr

What word stood out to you? Having presence is similar to the way you noticed the word *camel*. In the midst of the plain and ordinary, the person with presence stands out. Presence is what every speaker wants to exhibit on stage. It means you fully occupy the space. Observers get the feeling that you *own* it. Presence means people take notice of you and are in anticipation of what you will say or do next. How do you develop presence?

Be Alert

Be aware of what's going around you and what's happening inside you. If the class has not yet settled down to listen, sometimes just a steady look at the students who are not ready is enough to give them the signal to be still. Be in the moment. Don't think about the video game you're going to play tonight or the homework you didn't do yesterday. All your focus should be on the task at hand.

Physical Surroundings

Stand where you can be seen. This may mean changing the place where you were initially asked to deliver your speech. If there is a podium or a large microphone, make sure your face is not obscured by it. Try to seat people close together. The space around you affects the way the message is received. Hearing a person speak is not a passive event the way reading a book or watching a TV show can be, so use the space to your advantage.

Silence

Silence is more than the absence of noise. Silence can bestow authority and add influence and drama to a speech. Is there a statement to which you want the audience to pay attention?

Pause, saying nothing before you get to the key statement, speak it, then be silent for a beat after you've spoken it. Forgotten a word? Be quiet for a moment; the lost thought will return. Resist the impulse to mumble or fall into saying *um* or *er*. Standing silent and serene gives you poise and communicates presence.

Confidence

I know it can feel nerve-wracking facing all those people and trying to act like it doesn't faze you. Even though your knees are knocking, it's obvious you've got backbone because you're willing to try. That alone is proof that you possess confidence.

Knowing your subject matter imparts confidence, too. When you're speaking on a subject that's very familiar or that you have taken the time to study, this assurance in your knowledge shows through.

And you can always fake it to make it. If you don't feel all that self-assured, ask yourself the question: What actions would a confident person take? Then take those actions. Does the athlete crouch or raise her arms high when she scores? Does the beauty queen bow her head or hold it high as she promenades down the runway? Does the rock star strut or slouch his way across the stage? You do the same.

We assume that the brain is the boss of the body, but it can often work the other way around. If you hold your body in a way that takes up space, you send the message to others—including yourself—that you have control and confidence. In a study done by Dana Carney at the University of California, Berkeley, she found that adopting a power pose for sixty seconds yields the same amount of testosterone that you get after winning a game. (Testosterone is the same hormone some athletes use illegally to enhance their muscle strength.) In other words, positioning your body in a pose that is self-assured increases your sense of assurance even if you don't start out feeling that way. Your body will tell your brain "I've *got* this!" Pretty soon, your confident behavior will have you actually feeling confident.

Timing

Some speakers start off scared, but somewhere along the speech they really get into it and find themselves loving the spotlight. They keep talking on and on and on. They are fascinated with themselves—but the rest of us are in excruciating misery. It's like listening to a car alarm that can't be shut off. Don't get caught in that trap! It's easy to lose track of time, so designate someone to give you a signal to let you know when you only have a few minutes left. Otherwise, a perfectly good speech could be ruined because it went on a little too long.

Attitude

Attitude refers to the disposition and flair you bring to the speech. A speaker who captivates you has personality; she or he assumes a disposition that matches the message. There is a touch of the theatrical in the way he or she stands, moves, and talks. Suppose the topic is whether or not to allow students to use cell phones in school. You might mimic talking on a phone during the course of your talk. Maybe you're giving a report on French literature and you're able to use a French accent when making a particular point. Some people come by this quality naturally, while others have to cultivate it over time. Don't worry. As you grow more comfortable as a speaker, you'll be able to incorporate it into your speech.

Be Exciting, But Don't Do This

True or false? If a little bit of salt on my veggies is delicious, then a whole gallon of salt would make them taste even better. True or false? If children learn a lot in six hours of school a day, then sixteen hours of school a day would be better. If you've got even a teaspoon of brains in your body, you wouldn't fall for that logic, would you? Well, the same is true for speeches, too. You need to use good judgment. Something that might work in one situation doesn't always fit in another. For example, if the goofy thing you did in the locker room/at the dance/at the slumber party/when your parents weren't looking made everybody laugh, then the principal would think it's funny, too, right? I've never met your principal, but I've met plenty of principals in my day, and *no, no, no*, the principal would not find that funny.

I know you want your speech to be memorable and not boring. But it's important not to go to the extreme to make your speech exciting. Let me tell you about Kip.

I coached a poetry slam team, and "Kip" (not his real name) was one of the best performance poets. Kip was a clever, quick, and a snappy writer and a natural-born entertainer. For this particular competition, he wanted to read a poem he had written titled "Sexy Underwear." It was (as you might guess from the title) a racy poem about pretty girls. Kip delivered it with a lot of enthusiasm, and all the boys in the back of the class hooted and high-fived him after his performance. He sat down to lots of applause, but he was shocked when his score was the lowest one of the event. Why? Because his poem was totally inappropriate.

"That's not something you say at school," said the librarian, who was one of the judges. "That's what you say when you're at a party with your friends." And she was right. Match your talk to the audience and to the occasion. Not everything that's cool in one situation translates into another situation.

You can't play football with basketball rules—not if you want to win. You can't wear high heels on a mountain hike—not if you want to reach the top. And you can't say everything and anything if you want to win or reach the top. You might be the most hilarious joke-teller in the history of teenage joke-telling, but be advised that some of those jokes need to stay in the backyard and out of the school building. Comments that are in bad taste, remarks that ridicule other groups or individuals, clothing that is too revealing or inappropriate, statements whose *only* purpose is to shock—

will these wake up the snorers? Yes. Will people take note of your speech? Yes. But for all the wrong reasons. They get you noticed—but in a decidedly negative way. You want your speech to get attention, but not in a way that gets you into trouble or causes you to be ridiculed on YouTube till the end of time.

CHAPTER 10
What to Do When You Make a Mistake

"If at first you don't succeed, you're running
about average."
—*M. H. Alderson*

Something's going to go wrong. That's right, you can't avoid it. Even if you take all the suggestions I made in this book and practice your speech a jillion times, something is not going to go the way you planned it. Even though you are smart, well-spoken, and have such an adorable dimple when you smile, you are also still human, and therefore imperfect. And not only are you imperfect, but the world is an imperfect place. Anything might happen. The good news is you can anticipate and prepare for some of those "anythings" so that you can recover from them if they occur.

Gone *and* Forgotten
"Roses are red, violets are, um, er, let's see . . . violets are . . ."

All of a sudden you can't remember the next line. Or you glance down at your paper and you've lost your place. Every good speaker has had this happen at least once, so don't feel like you're Doofus McDummy. First, breathe deeply and calm down. Give your nerves some space to relax and there's a good chance the forgotten phrase will float back to the surface or your eyes will land on the right place on the paper. If you still can't grasp the line, tell the audience, "One moment, please." Or just be silent while you collect yourself. They'll be sympathetic. They'll be rooting for you because they know how miserable they'd feel if it happened to them. If you still can't recall the accursed line, go on from there to the next part. If it feels safe, you can make a joke about yourself and your jitters, then resume your talk. Do not go back to the very beginning of your speech. Pick up where you stopped and keep going.

Over and Under

You show up for the elementary school piano recital where you have graciously offered to be the MC, and you see that you're the only one in jeans while everyone else—even the kindergartners—are in suits. You enter the classroom to deliver your book report in your Sunday best, while all the other students are wearing their regular school clothes, so now you feel like a nerd. You picked the wrong thing to wear and it's too late to go home and change clothes. What now?

Go ahead and deliver your speech. Being overdressed or underdressed is a mistake and somewhat embarrassing, but it doesn't lead to a criminal conviction with time in jail. You're there to give a talk, so talk. If you want to poke fun at yourself about your clothing, you're allowed to do that, but don't focus on it too much. Just proceed with your speech.

Generally, it's less of a catastrophe to be overdressed than to be underdressed. If you look too stuffy for the occasion, you can lessen that image by being more casual in your speaking style. If you are too casually dressed, you may offer a brief apology for not being more appropriately dressed, or you can simply not comment so as not to draw more attention to your gaffe. It's up to you. In some circumstances, you might even be asked not to speak if your dress is extremely unfit. But most of the time the show will go on. The important thing is to do the speech and do it to the best of your ability. That is what will remove undue attention to your outfit.

Props and Audiovisual Equipment

I bet you didn't realize this, but when you're sleeping, the gadgets of the world are plotting ways to trick and torture humans. That's why your computer won't download the music program, you can't locate the app on your phone that you *know* is there, or the printer refuses to print out your homework. These machines are laughing at you behind your back.

When you give a presentation and are using props or audiovisual equipment, make sure you know how to operate it. Don't wait till that moment in your talk when you go to press the button and nothing happens to try and figure it out. Rehearse your speech using the video, PowerPoint, cue cards, easel, or whatever other aids you plan to have on hand. Even when you do know how everything works and you have rehearsed using the equipment, it may still fail. That's why I recommend thinking ahead on how you can cover the material without the use of the prop or machine, just in case. I'll give you more details about this in Chapter 12.

Supersized Nervousness

Some of you may be thinking: "You don't understand. I am *extremely* scared and *especially* jumpy when I have to stand up in front of a group. Really, really, really scared and very, very jumpy. I've got the kind of condition where I perspire so hard I have a waterfall of sweat cascading down my face and my voice turns into a quivering, quavering squeak."

Yes, there's help for you. Here's my prescription: Before your speech, make sure you are well prepared. Know your content, practice saying it aloud, and review your notes. Being well prepared will give you confidence. During your speech, remember to breathe. Inhale deeply. Get more oxygen to your brain and in your lungs. Air really does have speech-enhancing virtues.

If you know you tend to perspire, pack some tissues to bring along. In fact, if you perspire heavily, bring small paper towels; they don't disintegrate as easily. Dab discreetly and keep talking. If you know your voice might crack or your tongue could get dry, bring along some bottled water. Use the restroom before you go onstage. That energy that's surging through the room can come to your aid as well.

Most people will be secretly sending you positive vibes to help you out. You may actually be able to sense their positive energy and draw upon it. Pick out a friendly face in the crowd and take strength from the knowledge that that person wishes you well. Tell yourself, "I can do it. I can get through this." And you will.

Jumping the Play

Once, I was in a play with four characters. It was an ensemble piece, meaning no one character was the lead—we all spent about the same amount of time onstage. The show ran three times each weekend, and after numerous performances I felt very grounded doing my part. However, on one occasion, when the show was over, the director grabbed me and shouted, "You jumped the play!"

"What?" I didn't even know what "jumped the play" meant.

"You jumped the play! You skipped over about three or four scenes and said a line toward the middle of the play," she explained.

Fortunately, the other actors were true professionals. They picked up from the place where I had jumped ahead and continued on with the show. They did it so seamlessly that I didn't even realize that fifteen minutes of the story had been left out. And I bet the audience didn't know either.

Mack the Knife

Because I know you are a unique and original person, there are other flubs, fumbles, and goof ups you might make that I haven't thought of. I can make you this guarantee: ideas for what to do will come to you in the moment. Sitting in your chair reading this book you may say to yourself, "Man, there's no way I could figure out something cool to do if I were in a pickle!" But trust me, your brilliant little brain will unpickle you.

Allow me to digress for a moment and give you a musical history lesson. Have you ever heard of scat singing? It's a style of jazz singing where you don't sing actual words, you sing nonsense syllables that complement the sound of the musical notes. One night, jazz singer Ella Fitzgerald was performing the song "Mack the Knife." (I know you've never heard of it, but ask your grandmother, she'll remember it). Midway through the number, she forgot the words. Blanked out. Zippo. She was onstage, performing in front of a crowd that had paid good money to see her. So what did she do? She just made up some syllables and sounds and sang them to the melody. The audience thought she was scat singing on purpose. They didn't know it was an accident. They thought it sounded hot and jazzy. Ella Fitzgerald ended up winning a Grammy award for her rendition of "Mack the Knife." As a result of her mistake. Did you get that? *She won a Grammy, the highest award in the music industry—for goofing up.*

Oh, but she's a great singer and she wasn't delivering a speech, you say. I can't just start scat speaking my history report and expect my teacher to go for that.

Okay, I have another story to tell you.

Are you familiar with Maya Angelou? She was the author of several autobiographies and the poet who performed at the invitation of President Clinton for his Inauguration Day program. In other words, she was a heavy-duty poet.

I have a videotape of her reciting one of her poems, "Still I Rise," which I like to show my students. After we watch her performance, which she did with a lot of verve and style, I give the students a copy of the poem so they can read along while they watch the tape a second time.

On the second hearing, they discover that she made an error. She misses an entire stanza of her own poem. But unless you had the poem in front of you, you probably wouldn't guess it. When they view the tape a second time, they notice a brief hesitation where, if you know to watch for it, you see where she realizes that she's made a boo-boo, but she recovers smoothly, then proceeds with the poem. Despite the mistake, the audience is obviously enjoying her performance and applauds her warmly and with enthusiasm when she ends.

I tell you these stories to drive home the point that yes, you *will* come up with something if you make a mistake. You can always learn from your mistakes. If nothing else, you'll know what *not* to do next time. Every *uh-oh* can become an *aha!*

Try This

Just for fun, listen to "Mack the Knife" by Ella Fitzgerald from the album *Ella in Berlin* or any other song that features scat singing. Now play one of your favorite songs, but don't sing the words. Try scatting them.

CHAPTER 11
How to Improve Your Speech without Changing a Word

"Strategy is better than strength."
—*Hausa proverb*

Your nose is inside your tongue. I'm not saying that to gross you out. But it's true; your nose and your tongue are practically intertwined. You already know that your taste buds help you tell the difference between pretzels and sweet potatoes. They're set on fire by jalapeño peppers and they pucker up with a bite of sour pickles.

But your taste buds are not the only part of your body doing the tasting. Your sense of smell has a powerful influence on how things taste. If you've ever had a cold and your nose was stopped up, you may remember you probably lost your appetite. Why? Because you couldn't smell, so your food didn't taste right. How well your nose works affects how good your food tastes. In fact, what we describe as taste is really a flavor combo of taste, aroma, texture, and visual presentation.

In the same way, a speech is not just the words spoken. It is the combination of a variety of nonverbal elements that determine whether your speech is good or not. Paying attention to these other ingredients will improve your speech.

What I'm going to tell you next are some of the secrets that the best speakers know. Delivering a good presentation demands that you make your best effort; that you take the time to organize your thoughts, practice your talk, and pay attention to your pace, posture, and the pitch and tone of your voice.

But there are other things that have very little to do with your performance that can make it better. Lean in closer and I'll tell you what they are.

Come Closer

That last sentence in the previous paragraph was a clue. Having people seated physically close to you—and to each other—makes them feel like you've delivered a better speech than if you had delivered the exact same speech but they were scattered all over the room. Why is that? Remember when I talked about the ball of energy I feel when I have to speak? Well, there's a field of energy among the people in the room, too. Remember when I said that the people in the audience want to feel connected to you, the speaker? They also want to experience connection with each other. Human energy is contagious. Having everyone in close physical proximity boosts that flow of energy from one person to the other. Your jokes become funnier because laughter is contagious; if one person laughs, the person close by is likely to start laughing, too. Sitting close to one another changes the audience from a room of separate individuals into a gathering of souls sharing a common experience.

Encourage people to move to the front and to fill in the empty seats. I think people don't like to sit in the front row because they're afraid if the program is dull they can't easily sneak out. But there's no need for them to worry about that because you're going to have them spellbound. Tell them to "C'mon down." They might grumble at first, but they'll be glad they came closer once the program gets going and they feel that dynamic flow.

Pssst . . .

You already know that you have to vary the loudness and softness of your diction to keep them listening. If you really want them to pay close attention . . . whisper. Save one of your important points to deliver *sotto voce* (SOT toe VO chay)—that's Italian for "in a low voice." Maybe you've had a teacher or two who was wise enough to know that screaming at a bunch of screaming kids isn't the best way to communicate with them. Whispering to the class is more effective at grabbing their attention, because whispering is such a contrast to the noise, so it makes people stop, look, and listen. Just make sure your whisper is a stage whisper.

In other words, although you're talking low, you still have to project so that your whispered words can be heard.

We Like Mike

A lot of people don't like to use a microphone. It isn't always necessary, but when it is necessary, it's really necessary. Too often, an inexperienced speaker will decide that the microphone seems too artificial, huge, and clunky and it would be so much simpler to just talk loudly. The problem with that is you may start out projecting, but as the speech goes on, you could easily fall back into a more moderate volume—and then your audience can't hear you. When should you use a mike? If you have a big room, a big group, and especially if you have a soft or trembling voice, use the mike.

Before the presentation starts, do a mike check. Speak into the mike ("Testing—one, two, three") to judge how close you need to be to get the best sound, how to avoid feedback (that's the awful squawk you hear when the microphone is poorly adjusted), whether or not the mike can be moved, and how to turn it on and off.

Eye to Eye

Yes, we're back to eye contact. I don't know why so many people are squeamish about looking folks in the eye when this one thing tends to make people feel more sympathetic and empathetic to the speaker. If you want them to like you, give them the eye. Meeting a person's gaze is a way of communicating that feels more personal. Increased eye contact is almost always effective.

Zzzz . . .

Get a good night's rest the day before you speak. Well-rested speakers feel better, look better, and perform better. Speaking takes stamina. It may look like a preacher, teacher, actor, lecturer, or motivational speaker is just standing there and chit chatting, but there are a lot of skills at play. The person who has gotten sufficient rest has the reserves of energy to step up to the plate, or rather to the platform. Feeling frazzled only increases your nervous tension and isn't the type of energy that fuels your fire. Zzzzs are the hidden help that add zest and zip to your delivery.

Desire

Often, wanting something powerfully enough helps you to achieve it. I had some of the *baddest* poets in Washington, D.C., ready to sling words for the poetry slam. The students had written good poems, rehearsed their words, and were set to go. I was feeling strong and positive about their abilities and told them so—not because I was trying to build them up, but because I really believed it.

We got to the competition and met a team that was steady and ready, too. We matched them poem for poem and the score was close. It made us a tad nervous, but hey, we were grand poets, great speakers, and had good luck. We knew we weren't going to lose.

We lost.

We went home disappointed and shocked. What had we done wrong? Actually, nothing. Sometimes that's just the way life goes. But what it did was motivate us to polish our poetry, strengthen our speaking skills, and work our show with as much magic as we could muster.

The next competition, we won.

What made the difference? I can't point to any one thing. Most of the poems we used in the second contest were the same ones we used in the first one. All of the people who spoke in the first contest were the same people in the second. But having lost the first time we had a point to prove that next time. We wanted it badly that second time. Desire and determination, backed by our hard work, are what made the difference. They can make the difference for you, too, even when you're not in competition. Be enthusiastic, be committed, desire success, then focus on the success you desire, and quite likely you'll succeed. You don't have to be facing an Olympic battle to benefit from heartfelt determination. In many cases, that enthusiasm and attention will direct your actions—both consciously and unconsciously—to do what you need to do to be at your best.

Short and Sweet

If you have a choice between including lots of information for a longer lecture or cutting something out and running a little short—be brief. It's better to leave them thinking "I'd have loved to have heard more" rather than "When will this be over?"

You may want to take your wristwatch off and lay it on the podium or put your phone where you can keep track of your time. Or you may place a friend at the back of the room to hold up a sign signaling when you have five minutes left so that you won't run over the allotted time. When you see people in the audience fidgeting or stealing glances at the clock, those are clues that you've gone on long enough and should bring your remarks to a close. It's usually better to be too short than to be too long. KISS the audience goodbye— Keep It Short and Sweet.

CHAPTER 12

Using Audiovisual Equipment and Other Props

"Never let a computer know you're in a hurry."
—*Anonymous*

Girl. Guy. Gadget. People and props. Humans and high-tech. Sometimes speakers stand in front of an audience all alone. And sometimes they use audiovisual aids of one sort or another to help enhance their message. The trick is to make sure that the technology you use actually adds to and doesn't take away from the speech. How do you do that? By knowing how to operate the equipment, making sure that the equipment is good to go, and choosing the right tool for the job. Each type of technology has its own quirks, so let's look at how to deal with them.

Don't Leave the Microphone Alone

I used to resist using a microphone. I had a voice that could reach the back of the room (in other words, I had a big mouth), so I assumed everyone could hear me. And they could—as long as I was talking in a classroom or to a small group of people. But in an auditorium or in a space with a large number of people, more amplification is required.

If you're speaking behind a podium, the microphone will probably be mounted on a stand. Angle the head of the microphone so that it is about five inches from your mouth. Of course, you'll arrive early to check that the mike is working. "Testing—one, two, three." Hearing that awful *squawk* is irritating, so try not to subject your audience to that.

Experienced speakers sometimes leave the podium and walk through the crowd while talking. This is easier when the mike is handheld, meaning no cord is attached to it. If there is a cord, take note of how long it is (another reason to arrive early). This will determine how far you can stray away from the lectern (another term for podium). Sometimes when you walk away from the podium and move nearer to the audience, it makes them feel closer to you. That makes them enjoy you and your talk all the more. On the other hand, it may make more sense to stay put rather than to repeatedly walk two inches away only to be stopped short like a puppet on a string. If you have a long cord, you should practice a little with it, too. (See, a third reason to come early.) To prevent tripping over the wire, practice flicking the cord so that it lands behind you and out of the way of your feet.

If you are appearing on television, you will probably wear a lavalier, also known as a lav or lapel mike. The lav is a tiny microphone that won't be very noticeable. The technician will string the microphone's cord under your clothing so it can't be seen, then clip the actual microphone to your shirt collar or lapel. If you're wearing ruffles, or a large, clunky necklace, you need to be still because if there's too much movement, you'll brush up against the mike and make rustling or jangling sounds. Other than that, forget about the mike's presence. There's no need to lean toward it or angle your mouth into it.

Video

Let's cut to video! So you want to show a film clip or video as part of your presentation. In advance, load the DVD or cue up the digital file to the beginning of the section you are showing. That way, all you have to do is confidently press Play and you're set. No unpleasant surprises where you learn too late that you've got the wrong video or you're in a frantic panic, repeatedly hitting rewind and fast-forward trying to find the right place.

Dimming the lights a little might enhance viewing, but don't make it completely dark. Darkness can be a distraction, leading some to become drowsy or become mischievous because they think the speaker can't see them.

In Front of the Camera

Maybe you want to *be* in a video. Lots of people make videos at home that they upload to the Internet. Just because you're speaking in your bedroom doesn't mean it's not public speaking. When you set up, make sure the area that is visible in the shot is free of clutter. Yes, this means you might have to clean up your room—or at least the corner that will be seen on camera. If you include a graphic, make sure the words or pictures are large, legible, and have lots of white space around them. Otherwise, it may look too busy and won't be easy to read.

Before you start shooting, get very quiet. Can you hear the air conditioner humming? Is that the sound of a radio playing in another room? Are there heavy traffic or construction noises that you can hear indoors? You may have to turn off some appliances or machinery, or film in a different place to prevent those noises from leaking into your video.

How you dress is important on video, just as it is in person. Solid colors are easier on the eyes than patterns. A medium blue works well for many people. And make sure the color you wear doesn't blend into your backdrop. If you are standing in front of a green wall and you're wearing a green shirt in the same shade of green, that's not a good combination. It will look like your head is levitating all by itself in a green black hole.

Try This

Note what TV news anchors wear—colors or prints? What colors dominate? Tune in to a sitcom you haven't watched before. What does the "smart" character wear? What does the "goofy" character wear? How can these observations guide you in what you choose to wear on camera?

PowerPoint

A PowerPoint presentation (or a Keynote presentation, for all you Mac users, or a Google Slides presentation) is a computer-based slide show. Not only can it display slides and still photos, it can also incorporate videos and music.

Most people don't take advantage of all these capabilities; they simply use the PowerPoint as a large electronic set of index cards. And that is so drab and dreary it makes me want run out of the room. It makes me want to scream. It makes me want to jump up and down and spin in circles like a Tasmanian devil. Anything to relieve the tedium! (Okay, okay, I'm going to calm down now.) Nobody wants to read your notes projected on a big screen.

Your job is to deliver a speech, not read your outline out loud. If you're talking about the solar system, rather than showing a list of the planets on a slide, show a photograph of each planet as you discuss it. Rather than only talking about your favorite actor, upload a clip from the movie that made him a star. The advantage of PowerPoint is that it can add sound, color, and motion to your presentation. If people wanted to read a lot of text, they could get the information you're giving them from a textbook.

Of course, some text is a part of the presentation. For the text that you do use, make sure you use a large enough font, usually 26- to 32-point font size for the words and 36 to 44 for headlines. The words should be in a contrasting color to the background for ease of viewing.

Cell Phone

Don't use it. I will personally come to the front of the room and take it out of your hands if I catch you taking a call or sending a text during a presentation. Once, I was leading a Double Dutch team that was doing an exhibition in front of scores of people. One of the rope turners heard her phone ringing. The phone was in her purse, stashed off to the side of the stage. When she heard the phone, she stopped turning, abandoned the jumper in the middle of her go, and left the people watching wondering *what?* when she went to answer the call. How rude! I never had her on my team again.

Unless you need it to look at the time, don't bring your phone to the podium. And if you do have it with you, turn it off. We do not want to hear your favorite song or your blaring ringtone when your phone goes off. Don't even set it to vibrate, because if a call triggers the vibration, you'll be tempted to look at it and get distracted. Turn it off.

Before you start speaking, ask the people in the audience to turn off their phones, too.

The Back Channel

I know you love your i-Thingy, your tablet, and your complicated computerized watch. But unless you're reading notes on your device, you need to leave Gadget World behind you when you're behind the podium.

It can be distracting if you're trying to make eye contact with someone whose eyes are locked on a screen. It's disheartening to realize that the group's focus is somewhere off in cyberspace. Conversely, it can catch you off guard when you state a fact and someone immediately looks up that statement online and challenges you on it. This interaction online while you're speaking up front is called the back channel.

Try to get your audience to disconnect from the e-universe. As compelling as being connected can be, it's wiser—and more satisfying—to be front and center, human to human, giving and receiving in the moment. Command your moment.

Keep in mind that you're not always going to be able to do that. People may be surreptitiously (or defiantly) checking in with their devices. I went to a performance at Carnegie Hall in New York City. There was a prominent sign on the door prohibiting all cell phone use. But some people pulled out their phones anyway—and whenever someone was foolish enough to do so, the usher swooped down on that person and forced him or her to Turn. It. Off. *Now.* Those ushers had eagle eyes and did not take "no" for an answer. However, you won't have a personal anti-phone police force to control your classmates. So what should you do?

At the beginning of your speech, remind people to turn off their electronics. Try to save any mentions of websites or social media sites you need to reference for the close of your talk. Have them listed on the last slide of your presentation.

Some real-time, online, in-person interaction can be fun, if it's a planned part of your presentation. You just need to make sure people don't get entranced by their phones and forget all about you, standing there in living color.

Handouts

Paper handouts are old school but still useful. The main thing is timing. Often, an eager-to-help classmate will offer to pass out your handouts at the beginning of your talk. Tell your eager-pleaser friend, "Thanks, but no thanks." Unless you plan to refer to the papers at the beginning of the program, it is best to save them for later. If you pass them out early, your classmates will look at them and not at you. What's better is to distribute the papers when you actually want the audience to do an activity on the paper or read an item along with you.

For example, if you're giving a quiz that will lead to a discussion as you give each correct answer, the time to pass out the quiz is when you reach test time in the talk. In most other cases, the best time to give students handouts is at the conclusion of your presentation.

How do you decide whether to use handouts or an electronic presentation? If you want people to take notes, do a pen-and-paper activity. If you want them to have a souvenir of the talk—use handouts. If you want them to be engaged by sound and movement or digest ideas in a group experience, use a computer.

Props

Will a demonstration be part of your presentation? Maybe you're going to do something elaborate like a magic trick or science experiment that requires several tools or materials. Or maybe you're doing something simple that only requires that you hold up an object. Either way, practice making your remarks as you manipulate the prop so that you can do it with ease. Have someone watch you do it to give you feedback from the audience's point of view. As you're demonstrating something, you may need to stand behind or to the side so that your face is not obscured. You may have to work things slightly differently or even in reverse to how you normally do it in order for your classmates to see with an unobstructed view. You might consider making your motions slow and deliberate to make sure everyone in the class can see the item or the process. Because you know all about it, there's a tendency to rush through before the people watching can appreciate what you're doing.

F Is for . . .

Now that you know how to work all the equipment, what else do you need to know? How to do the speech *without* any of the equipment. That's right, because at any moment—usually at the worst possible moment—the equipment will cause you to fall victim to one of the Four Frightening F's: flub, failure, forget, and fluke.

A flub is a minor mishap, when some part of the process messes up. The clicker won't advance the PowerPoint past the seventh slide. The photocopier makes black streaks on the handouts. These things are nuisances, but they don't stop the show. Maybe you won't get an *A*, but you won't go home in shame, either.

A failure is when something won't work at all. The computer won't turn on, the ancient tape snaps into ribbons and becomes unplayable. The magic trick bombs and everyone can see how it's done.

To forget means that you or somebody else didn't remember to do or to bring something necessary. The handouts get left at home or nobody told the IT person to set up a laptop.

Then there are times when the big F happens: the fluke. A fluke is when something goes wrong for some crazy reason that no one could have predicted. That's what happened to Mary.

Mary's Scary Story

Mary is a speaker and trainer who gives workshops all over the country. One time, she was supposed to deliver a talk at a school. She had a PowerPoint presentation on her flash drive that she had formatted on her PC. She got to the place and clicked her flash drive into the school's Mac computer. Nothing happened. It didn't work. Her flash drive was supposed to be compatible with both Mac and PC platforms but for some crazy reason known only to the computer gremlins, it wouldn't cooperate. So the school went and got her a PC. That one didn't work, either. Then they sent for the tech guy and he got the computer working, but the LCD projector wouldn't operate.

But Mary wasn't flustered. She had her speech written out on paper and was able to deliver it from her notes. The show went on. She gave her talk without all the high-tech frills. Because she was prepared, she was able to go forward and do fine. She was able to defeat the Four Frightening Fs because she was able to apply the Triple As: anticipate problems, adapt to the situation, then move on ahead.

Let's break down the Triple As.

Anticipate: What could go wrong? Take time to think about this, not to increase your worry, but so that you can prepare and make a plan to address any glitch that comes up. Be like Mary. One of the things I do to be Mary-ish is I typically carry two copies of my notes. I also decide how to do my presentation with or without the use of a device.

Adapt: Know that not every circumstance is going to fit your plan A. You have to change to fit the situation at hand. Adjustability is your ally. I work as a trainer, and I was once asked to deliver a training workshop on time management for new employees. However, once I got started, the participants revealed that rather than feeling that they had problems with time and attendance, they had more concerns about finding reliable child care that would allow them to have good time and attendance at work. So I shifted the conversation to talking about ways the people in the room could become a secondary support system for one another. Creating the space to share that information proved more useful to my audience than sticking to the script.

Move on Ahead: One foot in front of the other carries you forward. Similarly, one word after the other moves your presentation forward. Keep going. If it goes badly, learn from the mistake and use it to be better prepared next time.

CHAPTER 13
When You Are Not the Speaker: Listening

"There is only one rule to become a good talker—learn how to listen."

—*Anonymous*

Becoming a better speaker can help make you a better listener, too. Now that you see how much goes into preparing and delivering a message, I expect that you'll naturally improve your listening skills. Many people mistakenly think listening is an easy, passive, humdrum way to kill time. *Au contraire!* Listening is an activity that requires effort and attention, but it is well worth it. And the better you are as a listener, the better you become as a speaker. It's a mutual admiration society between speaking and listening. When you appreciate listening well, you craft your own presentations in a way that respects the effort and patience that listeners offer when they are listening to you. Listening to other speakers helps you discover what to applaud and what to avoid. Let me lay out some of the benefits of good listening.

Hear Ye, Hear Ye!

First, students who pay attention are ahead in the homework game. You'd like to spend less time on homework, wouldn't you? Well, if you are focused and alert while the presenter is presenting, you are more likely to absorb the information, meaning you will spend less time at home working it out. So, don't doodle during Ms. Jackson's fifth period class tomorrow afternoon, and you won't have to struggle trying to complete Ms. Jackson's homework assignment tomorrow night.

Second, making a point to listen will allow you to learn so much more than when you give half an ear to what's going on. If your mind is on what's in the cafeteria for lunch, you're going to miss the three important points the speaker is outlining. Point number two might be the very thing that will (a) help you pass the test on Thursday, (b) turn you on to an entertaining website, or (c) provide you with the words that will impress the love of your life. Don't smirk; you don't know if you don't listen. So listen up.

Once, in class, we were discussing the work of poet Nikki Giovanni. The name *Nikki*, also spelled "Nicky," is a popular name for both boys and girls. Nikki Giovanni is a woman, but I had a boy in class whose name was also Nicky: Nicky Washington. On this particular day, my student Brittany came to my desk and commented that she really liked Nicky Washington. She meant to say "Nikki Giovanni." She made this remark after most of the students had left the room, so fortunately she didn't embarrass herself in front of everybody. But as luck would have it, Nicky Washington was one of the last people to leave the classroom, and I saw him register her remark, although Brittany herself had not realized what she had said. I was not surprised to notice a few days later that Nicky and Brittany were sitting together in the cafeteria almost every day. It paid off for Nicky that he was listening.

Learn to listen with your eyes as well as your ears. When you're listening, your ears aren't the only parts of you that are at work. Your eyes are tracking the nonverbal messages, reading gestures and interpreting facial signs. Only seven percent of any communication is with the words alone. If you're not watching as well as listening, that means that over 90 percent of what's going on is shooting past you like a jet plane. I remember talking with a lady who was supposed to be helping me with a writing project. "Will we be able to meet next week?" I asked her.

"Oh, yes. That will be fine," she said. "It'll be no problem." But as she said it, her voice was tight, and she was actually shaking her head no slightly. So when next week arrived and she canceled the appointment, I was not surprised. I already had someone in mind as a backup.

When you're speaking, you'll have to make a backup plan in the moment as you observe the audience and decode the nonverbal messages they are sending you. Do you sense a feeling of warmth or a friendly spirit in the room? You've got a great audience; keep doing what you're doing. A disconnect with the crowd will be registered by their lack of eye contact with you. When an audience is cool to me, I actually feel a shiver. That's a sure clue that I'm not connecting. Are your listeners restless? You'll have to say or do something to capture their interest. Perhaps you are reading too much from your notes. Stop reading and talk with the audience. Maybe you've gone on too long and need to proceed immediately to the close. "Listening" to the nonverbal behavior saves you from embarrassing situations and strengthens your morale.

Listening 101

Here are some of the moves that help you be an effective listener—you'll notice that some of them are the same tools you need to be a good speaker. Posture helps. Sitting up and facing forward, instead of leaning back and slumping down, gets your mind and body in position to hear and receive. Your good posture also shows the speaker you're going to be a receptive audience. I don't have to tell you how unsettling it is to look out into a sea of indifferent, unfriendly people. If those people are sitting there like sullen, lazy slugs, it makes it terrifying to stand and deliver. Don't do that to your fellow classmate.

It helps if you come to the talk without a lot of preconceived ideas. You may have studied the American Revolution in third grade, but when Mr. Coleman starts his unit on it, don't make the mistake of thinking you know all there is to know about the Declaration of Independence, Paul Revere, and the Boston Tea Party. Maybe the first time you were taught about the colonial era you didn't hear about Crispus Attucks or Molly Pitcher or Joseph Brent. When your classmate, the school nerd, stands to give a report on anime, don't groan and decide he's going to be a big bore. Hey, he may have read Chapter 8 and knows how to spice up a speech. You can learn from him, too. If you're such an expert on anime, what do you know about Osamu Tezuka?

Try This

Just for fun, show me just how much you *do* know about the Revolutionary War period. Without looking anything up, write a word or two about the following people:

Crispus Attucks   _____

Molly Pitcher   _____

Joseph Brent   _____

And how much do you know about anime? What is the difference between anime and manga?

_____

Who is Osamu Tezuka?   _____

_____

Now look up information about one of the topics above. What new things did you learn?

We tend to prejudge the speaker as well as the content. Some of us may like the girls better than the boys. Others give more weight to the things that men say over women. All of us tend to respond more favorably to the people who seem just like us or to those we consider to be good looking, popular, or cool. But there are things to be learned when we listen to everyone with an open mind. Most people tend to listen more closely to the beginnings and the endings of messages. But after all you've learned about what goes into a speech, you know that there's a lot of important information in the middle, too. You know that it'll be worthwhile to concentrate throughout the whole talk.

One of my favorite speakers is storyteller Donald Davis. The first time I heard him, he was on the roster with several other storytellers—a Native American teller and an African American teller. I love both American Indian folklore and black southern tales so I was primed to listen enthusiastically to those speakers. Then I saw that Davis was listed as an Appalachian storyteller. Ho-hum! I thought. Who wants to hear some hillbilly yarns? But Davis mesmerized me with his stories! I was completely captivated by his folktales and childhood memories, tall tales and wise words. I spent a boatload on his recordings and have used his books when I teach. Whenever he comes to my town, I'm the first person to buy a ticket.

I'm city born and bred and assumed I had no common ground with someone from Appalachia. I was prepared to dismiss him. But had I dissed him, I would have missed out on the wonderful, heartwarming, tear-jerking, thought-provoking messages he had to share. So put aside your preconceived judgments. Open your ears; your heart and mind will follow.

When listening to a speaker, you should be quiet and attentive. No talking, no texting, no hiding out in the back of the room. Try not to get caught up in whatever visual aids the speaker is using; don't pay more attention to the technology than to the talk. For example, if the speaker mentions a website, don't immediately check out that site while the speaker is speaking. Resist the urge to send comments via text to your friend on the other side of the auditorium. Once you start these interactions, you're no longer present for the speaker. For the person who is trying to speak, it feels like all the people in the audience have evaporated from their bodies and there's nothing left in the room but a bunch of androids.

Encourage fellow listeners to be respectful, too. Being in the same space as the speaker or performer is *way* different than watching something on the Internet or TV. The computer doesn't care if you snort, walk around the room, or make smart remarks. The television is oblivious if you talk back to it, make a phone call, or change the channel. But it makes a big difference to the human being who's trying to talk. When I stand in front of an audience, I can feel the mood of the people in the audience. I can sense tension, impatience, or indifference. When waves of those emotions are coming at me, it makes talking to those people tough. Fortunately,

I more often feel emotions like anticipation, curiosity, and congeniality emanating from them.

There have been times when I have been in a bad mood and standing in front of a crowd was the *last* thing I felt like doing. But the positive vibes I felt cascading over me as I spoke helped lift my mood. I am in a performance poetry group called The Spoken Word. Once, we were invited to perform at a recreation center, and I said yes because a good friend had asked me, but I really did not want to be there. It had been a long while since the group had done a show, plus I was tired. Tired of doing the same old material, tired of organizing the group and getting us together for rehearsals, and tired because it had been a long day. As I was sitting backstage waiting for our name to be called, I said to myself, "This is my last show ever. The fun has gone out of it for me." I resigned myself to doing it one more time and felt glad that after that night I wouldn't have to be bothered again.

Imagine my surprise when I stepped onstage and looked into the audience. I saw children looking back at me with happy expectation. Their faces read, "What's about to happen next? What fun thing are you going to do?" I saw my friend smiling at me, tickled that I had said yes to her request. I looked at my fellow performers, excited to sing, play, and recite, presenting these gifts they were delighted to share. With all that exhilaration coming at me, I fell in love with being on stage all over again. That was over ten years ago, and since then I've done loads of poetry performances, history lectures, and training workshops, and it's still gratifying. That energy renews itself each and every time.

I hope that you send waves of love to the kid whose knees are knocking as he tries to speak at the assembly. Your respectful attitude supports the speaker's ability to do a good job and contributes to the spread of a harmonious spirit in the room. What goes around, comes around—if you spread good energy when someone else is the speaker, you're more likely to get it back when it's your turn.

Try This

Think about a time when you felt truly heard by another person. What did they do that made you feel understood? Who did most of the talking?

Don't Yawn, Listen

What do you do when the speaker is a bore? You still have to be courteous and respectful. A dull talker doesn't give you a free pass to pass notes—either on paper or via text. It doesn't mean you get to act mean to the poor kid who is dying in the front of the class because she hasn't yet learned how to handle her speech jitters. You have to sit through it politely. Is there anything you can do to make it end sooner? Not much, but you can try a few subtle things. When it's time to ask questions, don't ask any. Keep a blank expression on your face so that he or she is getting the feedback that the audience is not responsive and he or she can make an adjustment. Hopefully, someone in charge will signal to her to wind it up.

Just be kind and be patient. It will be over soon enough. And the speaker still deserves some applause when finished.

One of the best ways to show respect is by listening. Everyone has something to say, but so few people take time to genuinely hear one another. By becoming a fine listener, not just in the auditorium but in your interactions with other people, you will discover that your popularity will grow, others' esteem for you will increase, and their regard for you will deepen. You will have achieved a double bonus as someone who can both speak well *and* listen thoughtfully. Wonderful, worthy payoffs are waiting for the person who learns to listen and listens to learn.

CONCLUSION:
Stage Fright, BFF

"To me, fearless is living in spite of those things that
scare you to death."
—*Taylor Swift*

Right now, I wish I were you. You've just made a new friend
and your new friend is going to take you to exciting
places. You're going to have a lot fun and you're going to win
lots of praise and admiration. As with any new friendship, it
may take a while to get used to one another. But don't worry—
you'll become comfortable with each other over time. A good
friend can expose you to a side of yourself you didn't know
you had and cause you to grow in all areas of your life.

Now that you're improving your speaking skills you
can look forward to better grades, increased confidence,
and maybe more popularity. Solid speaking skills will be
useful to you once you're an adult, too, serving you well in
job interviews and getting you noticed by the people who can
promote you and offer other professional opportunities.

There are the obvious jobs that require good speaking skills: teacher, DJ, politician, preacher, sales agent, attorney, broadcaster. But I'm going to be a scientist, you say. I'll spend my entire day in a laboratory. Or I plan on becoming a truck driver. No one will be riding with me cross-country. But if you can present well, it'll do you well. In an age where video cameras are ubiquitous, you the scientist, may be interviewed for a podcast, or you the truck driver, may decide to talk about your travels in a podcast. Everybody likes earning more money, but the cash doesn't drop into your lap. Your ability to speak persuasively may be the edge that you need to land the big paycheck.

But in this particular moment in your development, I'm thinking about you and your spirit. You remind me of the good guy in a movie or the superhero in an adventure story. Just like them, you are overcoming the odds and proceeding to a very happy ending. For the hero, the enemy is usually a very bad man sporting a bad attitude and shooting guns all over the place. But for you, the opposing force isn't bad. Strong, yes, and just a little scary, with a bit of the unknown thrown in for good measure. In your adventure, you know that the villain won't get top billing. You don't need supernatural powers. You have access to the super but natural power surge that you once thought was bad nerves. You have a secret weapon—the knowledge that stage fright is your friend.

Try This

Name two things you used to be afraid of but aren't anymore (for example, the dark, staying at home by yourself, riding a two-wheeler). Now add one more thing to that list.

Things I Do Not Fear:

1.

2.

3. Public Speaking

AND HOW ABOUT THIS?

I'd like to hear your speech-giving skills. Choose one of the following exercises, then record yourself doing it.

Favorite Tongue Twisters

How well can you articulate? Practice your ability to speak clearly, correctly, and with precision by wrapping your tongue around these twisters:

Red leather, yellow leather.
Red leather, yellow leather.

A brief break for breakfast.

Eddie admitted it and Addie eliminated it.

A work week is unique when you work in a New York boutique.

Three free throws.

Fred fed Ted bread.

She sells seashells by the seashore.

I saw a kitten eating chicken in the kitchen.

If a dog chews shoes, whose shoes does he choose?

Poetry Power and Story Glory

Ready to show off a bit? Use your oral interpretation skills to tell a story or perform a poem. Here are a few poems by young people for you to try out along with some fables. Put on your best once-upon-a-time voice and tell one of the following.

Performance Poetry

This poem is modeled after the poem "Mother to Son" by Langston Hughes.

Student to Teacher
by Naakoshie Mills

Well, Teacher, my life
aint been no glass of lemonade
It's been warm sour milk
full of tiring term papers
And too many pop quizzes
while you sit here and
Teach easily

I'm the one to pass the class.

No more late night parties or fun games
Just hours of studying,
just for you, Teach.

I work so hard and it never pays off.
Just more work for me and less patience for you.

And your quizzes are too, too hard.

And you've got the nerve to call me lazy.
Please, I worked too hard for this crap.

Life for me aint been no chocolate milkshake.

What do you know that adults have a hard time understanding? The following poem schools us old folks about a young person's insights.

Being Young
by Christa Madikaegbu

Because you're so old
You've forgotten:
> How to smile
> youthfully;
> How to imagine a possibility.

You say we're too young to understand:
> The beauty
> of an inexhaustible earth;
> The joy of living.

But surely we understand
what you don't:
> The difference between now
> and yesterday;
> The abstract tension of tomorrow.

You say we're too young to understand
what we don't know, but
we're old enough to understand
what you have forgotten.

Sometimes you just have to tell everyone how awesome you are. No shyness, just showboating in this poem!

Fly
by Jailyn Smith

I fly so high the angels can't even touch me
I'm so hot I'm sweating like herbal tea
In the winter time, reciting what I heard
When I go outside, I'm so cold I look like a frozen bird
My poem is lit—it's like fire
Knowing no one can surpass me, because I'm higher
I'm so cool everybody likes me
So cool that nobody wants to fight
Closing this poem, because poetry's my life
My skills are so sharp I'm like a pocket knife.

Fables

Fables are short stories that convey a lesson. Ever heard of Aesop's fables? He's not the only one who wrote short tales to teach truths. I've adapted a few fables and written two of my own. Let's start with Mulla Nasruddin. Mulla Nasruddin is a legendary character well-known in the East. A Mulla is a religious leader. Mulla Nasruddin's tales reflect shrewd thinking and sage humor.

The Mulla, The Pumpkin, and the Walnut
He was wise, he was foolish, he was like me, he was like you. He was Mulla Nasruddin. Once, Nasruddin took his leisure in a pumpkin patch. It was a crisp autumn day with a friendly fall breeze. He propped his head on a fat pumpkin, stretched out his long legs, and gazed up at the tall walnut tree that spread its umbrella of leaves over his head.

"Why would God grow a large pumpkin on a spindly vine along the ground?" thought Nasruddin. "Surely, it would make better sense to have pumpkins grow on strong, sturdy trees."

Just then, a walnut fell off a branch and plopped on Mulla Nasruddin's head.

"Oh! God is so much wiser than me. It would have been trauma and tragedy had that been a pumpkin instead of a walnut that fell on my head!"

Are You Sleeping?

It was late but not too late. A time when some might be up and about and some might be down and out. Mulla Nasruddin was relaxed and reclining on his sofa.

In walked his brother who said, "Nasruddin—are you sleeping?"

"What do you want?"

"I want to borrow some money," said his brother.

"In that case—yes, I'm asleep. And don't wake me up!"

Turkish Bath Math

After a long, hard day of hard, physical labor, Mulla Nasruddin went to the Turkish bath to refresh himself. His clothes were dusty, torn, and hanging off his frame. He wore the odor of weariness and sweat. The bath attendant took one look at Nasruddin's ragged and bedraggled appearance and barely spoke to him. But when Nasruddin left, the Mulla gave the attendant a most generous tip.

The next week, Mulla Nasruddin returned to the Turkish bath. This time he wore a robe woven with gold thread. His shoes were made from rich, soft leather. He wore the turban on his head like a crown. He had the bearing of a prince.

The attendant smiled and greeted him warmly.

He bowed low, then personally led him to the baths. He brought the Mulla perfumed soap and plush towels. When it was time to depart, Nasruddin tossed him one penny.

The attendant was shocked—and offended. "What about my tip?" he spluttered.

"This tip was for my first visit," explained the Mulla. "And that first tip was for this time."

These next stories have more modern themes. The first, *Advice for Mice*, is my adaptation of one of my favorite contemporary fables. The second story, *Tapping the Power*, is an original.

Advice for Mice

Momma Mouse came home to what seemed like an empty home. She looked in the living room; no little ones to greet her. She looked in the bedroom; nobody there. She found her three baby mice crouching and cowering in a small, dark corner in the back of the house.

"Why are you hiding?" she asked.

"There's a huge, hungry cat prowling around. We hid because we're frightened," the oldest baby mouse told her.

"I'll take care of that!" said Momma Mouse.

"But Momma Mouse, the cat has sharp claws. She could tear you into bits!" the middle baby mouse screamed.

"And Momma Mouse, that cat is so much bigger

than you. You could never beat her!" the babiest baby mouse cried.

"I know what to do," Momma Mouse declared and strode near the door. The three baby mice hovered behind her and shivered with fear because they knew that the big, mean cat was in the room.

Momma Mouse cracked the door open, then in a loud voice shouted, "BOW-WOW!
BOW-WOW!"

Every hair on that cat's body stood up in fright and then that cat fled like a demon was chasing her.
The mother mouse turned to her children and said, "And now you know why you need to learn a second language."

Tapping the Power

The storm came and the electricity went out. No radio, no videos, no video games. We were without Wi-Fi. The lights were dark, the TV was down, and the phone was off. It was digital death.

What will we do?

What can we do?

Let's talk.

We talked to each other. We listened to each other. We cracked jokes, we remembered old times, we talked about school, we complained about work, we wondered about life and life after life. There was a story told about everything: how to speak in French, wield a wrench, hit a ball, knit a shawl, handle snakes, juggle plates, pass the test, do one's best.

His story helped her decide how to do the homework. Her story showed him how to make some money. The old one helped the young one figure things out, and the baby in the family made everybody laugh.

It wouldn't have happened if the electricity hadn't gone out. It wouldn't have happened if we had had the power.

But we *did* have the power—the power of the tongue.

"Whatever you are, be a good one."
—*Abraham Lincoln*

ADDITIONAL RESOURCES

Read This

The Spoken Word Revolution (*Slam, Hip Hop & The Poetry of a New Generation*) by Mark Eleveld. Naperville, IL: Sourcebooks Mediafusion. (Note: contains some strong language.)

The Poetry for Young People series published by Sterling Publishing Company. Poetry by various poets.

View This

www.highschooldebate.org
www.poetryoutloud.org
www.poetryslam.com
www.thoughtco.com/what-is-a-debate-1857491\

SPEECH TERMS TO KNOW

ad-lib—to speak without prepared notes

applause—clapping to show a speaker appreciation, praise, or thanks

articulate—to form words clearly and precisely

anecdote—a short, amusing story about a real person or incident

antithesis—when two opposite ideas are put together to emphasize a concept

audience—the people who have gathered to hear a speech or watch a performance

A/V—abbreviation for audiovisual; the equipment used to project sound and/or pictures

back channel—the use of digital devices or social media at the same time as a speech is being presented

body language—the way information is conveyed by one's stance, physical movements, facial expressions, and gestures.

cadence—the rising and falling of voice; momentary changes in pitch

call and response—a style of presentation that allows the audience to answer or encourage the speaker as the presentation is being made

dais—the raised platform where the speaker is positioned

delivery—the manner in which a speech is done

diaphragm—a muscular partition separating the thorax from the abdomen; it plays a major role in breathing

elocution—the art of articulate and expressive speech

extemporaneous—spoken without advance planning or rehearsal; in speech contests, it is an event where contestants are given a limited time to research a current events topic and deliver a speech

eye contact—the practice of looking into the eyes of audience members during a speech

feedback—sound distortion from a microphone or amplifier

icebreaker—an introductory activity led by the speaker to establish a friendly or receptive atmosphere with the audience

impromptu—to speak without advance planning or rehearsal; in speech contests, it is an event where contestants are given a theme and within minutes they must deliver a speech about it

inflection—variation in the sound or tone of words

lavaliere—a small microphone usually attached to a speaker's collar; also known as a lav or lapel mike

lectern—the tall, narrow table behind which the speaker stands

Master of Ceremonies (MC/emcee)—the person onstage who coordinates a live performance or social occasion;

metaphor—a comparison in which an object or idea is used to suggest a likeness between two things

mic check/mike check—the test of the microphone to make sure it is working properly

nonverbal communication—the messages conveyed through one's physical presence without talking; *see* body language

panel presentation—a format where several people share the platform to speak on different aspects of a single topic

parallelism—forming phrases with a similar grammatical pattern in terms of structure, sound, or meaning

platform—the area where a speaker is positioned

podium—the stand behind which the speaker is positioned; *see* lectern

projection—the process of speaking with sufficient force and volume to be heard

prop—short for properties, the objects or materials used as part of a performance

Q & A—short for Questions and Answers, the period during a talk when listeners can ask the speaker for more information

show and tell—an instructional practice where students bring in an interesting object or personal belonging and talk about it before the class

simile—using the words *like* or *as* to make a comparison between two unlike things

sotto voce (SOT toe VO chay)—to speak in a stage whisper; literally means "in a low voice" in Italian.

stage—a raised platform where performers present a speech or a show

stage fright—the fear that may accompany speaking in public

stage whisper—speaking in a way that suggests a whisper, but the voice is projected so as to be easily heard

zebra—a horse with black-and-white stripes—but you already knew that. *Now go work on your speech!*

INDEX